CORPORATE FINANCE
THE BASICS

Corporate Finance: The Basics is a concise introduction to the inner workings of finance at the company level. It aims to take the fear out of corporate finance and add the fun in, presenting the subject in a way that is simple to grasp and easy to digest. Its aim is to explain – and demystify – the essential ideas of corporate finance, avoiding the heavy use of maths and formulae. The calculations and figures in the book are purely to illustrate fundamental concepts, appealing to readers' common sense, rather than stretch their ability to do "number-crunching".

Topics covered include:

- Financial statements through the corporate finance lens
- How to make investment decisions
- Cash versus profit
- Net working capital management
- How to determine the value of a business

Through the use of a subject map, this book explains how the key components of the subject are connected with each other, strengthening the reader's understanding. This book is the ideal introduction for anyone looking for a short yet scholarly overview of corporate finance.

Terence C.M. Tse is Associate Professor of Finance at ESCP Europe Business School. He teaches corporate finance at all degree levels and has run numerous executive training workshops around the world. In addition to his advisory role to the EU, Terence has provided commentaries on the latest current economic and financial affairs and market developments in newspapers, on television and on the radio. Before joining the world of academia, he worked in mergers and acquisitions at Schroders, Citibank and Lazard, and in UK financial services advisory at Ernst & Young. He obtained his doctoral degree from the Cambridge Judge Business School, University of Cambridge, UK.

THE BASICS

CORPORATE FINANCE

THE BASICS

Terence C.M. Tse

Routledge
Taylor & Francis Group

LONDON AND NEW YORK

First published 2018
by Routledge
2 Park Square, Milton Park, Abingdon, Oxon, OX14 4RN

and by Routledge
711 Third Avenue, New York, NY 10017

Routledge is an imprint of the Taylor & Francis Group, an informa business

British Library Cataloguing-in-Publication Data
A catalogue record for this book is available from the British Library

Library of Congress Cataloging-in-Publication Data
A catalog record for this book has been requested

ISBN: 978-1-138-69558-0 (hbk)
ISBN: 978-1-138-69560-3 (pbk)
ISBN: 978-1-315-52657-7 (ebk)

Typeset in Bembo
by Apex CoVantage, LLC

In loving memory of my parents

CONTENTS

FIGURES

TABLES

ACKNOWLEDGEMENTS

I would like to thank my wife, Dr Céline Druilhe, for having read the entire manuscript several times in various iterations and for providing generous comments and hints on how to improve its readability. She did it all without a single complaint. Without her perseverance and astonishing patience, this book would not have been possible. Thank you again; I could not have done it without you. I am also indebted to Lizzie Sabin for proofreading my book from start to finish; she has worked magic on it. I would additionally like to thank Andy Humphries and Laura Johnson at Routledge for all their assistance and their willingness to put up with me. Naturally, any defects that remain are mine and mine alone. Lastly, I would like to dedicate this book to my children, Clélia and Lucile.

FOREWORD

I have known Terence for many years. He has always been one who can explain matters in simple ways. This is why, when he told me that he was working on a book that presents corporate finance that is accessible to everyone and asked me to write the foreword for it, I was excited by both. The result is that he has managed to find a way to explain corporate finance in a simple and lively way that I did not think was possible before. Corporate finance is an evolving discipline with potentially infinitely complicated concepts. There are many, many corporate finance textbooks out there, one thicker than another, competing on which can show how to do the latest complicated derivative structure calculation. But those books often confuse and frustrate readers new to the subject who just want to get a basic understanding first, without ever wanting to become a derivatives engineer at a bank.

This book manages to highlight the key concepts without dwelling on them for too long and going into unnecessary detail, which keeps the read a fast-paced one, with content that is easy to digest for readers. It takes a solid understanding of corporate finance and many years of teaching experience to be able to distil the key fundamentals of corporate finance and show it in as simple terms as this book does. It is priceless for those picking up the subject for the first time, those from a non-finance background moving into more senior managerial roles in their companies, and even those who haven't had to do technical work in this area but who want a quick refresher.

Happy reading!

Alvin Miu
Chief Operating Officer and Chief Financial Officer,
MF Jebsen International

INTRODUCTION

As a finance professor, I frequently find myself in an unenviable situation: teaching new business students and executives who often tell me that they find the subject of corporate finance stupefyingly boring, intimidating and difficult – if not all three. This is especially the case when, for most programmes in business schools, it is a core and mandatory subject. Students' preconceived feelings towards corporate finance are usually confirmed when they get overwhelmed by financial concepts on the very first day of class. The risk is that they quickly fall behind, without ever obtaining a solid grasp of the basics. Consequently, some students find it difficult – if not impossible – to understand the more complex concepts as the course progresses. On top of this, there is no avoiding the calculations that accompany the concepts. For those who are not mathematically astute, corporate finance can be a nightmare, turning the learning process into a long, waterless march through the desert, rather than a pleasant hike in the Alps.

One would think that many books would be available on the market to help allay fears of the subject and to make it more engaging. The range is indeed wide. Some are loaded with technical and quantitative jargon right from the start and are far more suitable for those who know the field well. At the other end of the spectrum there is lighter fare, and those books are more accessible to novices – but many of them are too focused on accounting rather than finance.

There are also textbooks. Covering the subject comprehensively, they tend to be long-winded and contain too much detail. Arguably, they are often ill-suited to the needs of many managers, especially those who are *not* in finance roles. Frequently, these professionals want a book that gives them a comprehensive view on the subject but that does not bog them down with the technical details and calculations that are not pertinent to their jobs. They are far more interested in gaining an overview of the key concepts of corporate finance and how these relate to the business issues that they encounter on a daily basis.

THE PURPOSE OF THIS BOOK

Meeting these aforementioned needs is the rationale behind *Corporate Finance: The Basics*. It aims to focus only on the most essential concepts – enough for readers to pick up what is most important and relevant to their work – and leave out the nitty-gritty stuff. Any experienced manager will tell you that, in order to evaluate whether a project or action is successful, you need to be able to measure the outcomes. For readers of this book, the goal is this: if novices in the subject – students and professionals alike – can pick up the gist of what others are talking about in conversations about corporate finance issues, and even contribute to them, then this book has successfully delivered on its promise.

This book is therefore less concerned with the broader financial services industry, such as investment funds, derivatives and insurance or the financial markets themselves. Instead, it goes into more detail on the key topics of corporate finance, looking at how to manage the financial affairs of a company. A note before proceeding: even though the word "corporate" in corporate finance may suggest that the topic is only relevant to large businesses, this is not the case at all. Understanding corporate finance is just as important to large company CEOs as it is to entrepreneurs if they want to achieve economic success with their businesses.

OUTLINE AND STRUCTURE OF THIS BOOK

Chapter 1 starts by looking at accounting statements. Even though this book is about corporate finance, a discussion of financial statements is necessary, and indeed useful, for two reasons. First, they are what many managers frequently encounter in their day-to-day activities, particularly those with "P&L (profit and loss) responsibilities" (those who need to take care of the profitability of the business unit). Second, corporate finance borrows a great deal from financial statements. Therefore, understanding them is helpful for understanding financial management.

The key to the success of any company is to invest in the right opportunities and the right means of production, which, in turn, can make money for the investors. This is the starting point of Chapter 2, which examines how to make (the right) investment decisions and the various investment criteria methods.

Chapter 3 focuses on the idea of free cash flows as a measure of new value created by investment decisions. It also clarifies the difference between profit and cash – two concepts that can create much confusion for people who are new to corporate finance.

Chapter 4 delves into the oft-ignored but all-too-important subject of working capital management. Few people know what working capital is, let alone why it is so important to businesses. To explain these, the chapter looks at the concept of the cash conversion cycle, while demonstrating how working capital can be managed.

The subsequent two chapters discuss raising capital to take on investments.

Chapter 5 looks at debt capital by first examining what leverage is and how it works. It then discusses two types of debt – bank loans and bonds – as well as the costs of using these two instruments. Bonds are often ill-understood by beginners, so this chapter gives an overview of the basics of bonds.

Chapter 6 examines the characteristics and usage of share equity. It then looks at two methods for estimating the cost of using equity. Chapter 6 ends with a summary of the past two chapters by discussing the concept of weighted average cost of capital.

The emphasis of Chapters 7 and 8 is on mergers and acquisitions (M&A). Chapter 7 looks at the strategic rationale behind the numbers. It also examines the different types of M&A. Chapter 8 considers how companies are valued and introduces the three most common valuation methods. Throughout these two chapters, the book considers the topic of M&A from the perspectives of start-ups/ entrepreneurs, investment bankers, major corporations and buyout firms.

Chapter 9 summarises the main points discussed in the previous eight chapters by going through the "big picture" provided. It represents an attempt to show how the different aspects of corporate finance are connected.

Now that the path has been laid out, let's begin the journey!

FINANCIAL STATEMENTS

CHAPTER OVERVIEW

The three types of financial statement are not only the foundations of the subject of accounting, but they also serve as a good starting point for a discussion on corporate finance for at least two reasons. First, many of the concepts and ideas within corporate finance are effectively drawn from two other subjects: accounting and economics. So, it is natural to start the conversation with the foundation stones of accounting. Second, these financial statements reveal a significant amount of financial information that can help us manage a business and its financial affairs better. Even grasping the basics of these statements can help us to understand a great deal about the operational and financial state and the performance of a business.

INCOME STATEMENT

Before proceeding, it must be noted that – even though under specific accounting rules there are clear guidelines about how to treat the various items on these financial statements – here, we are more concerned with viewing these *accounting* statements from the vantage point of *corporate finance*. In other words, we are far more interested in what financial information we can extract from them than how to apply accounting conventions.

Revenue and costs

The income statement (also called the *profit and loss account*) measures the performance of a company over a period of time, usually a quarter or a year. An example of this type of statement is shown in Figure 1.1. Fundamentally, this document shows two main aspects of business: 1) what is left to the company after selling its products or services, and after all the costs have been subtracted, and 2) how what is left over is distributed among the investors.

At the top of the income statement is revenue (also called *sales* or *turnover*), which reflects how much money a company has made from selling a number of units of goods and services at the price that it can charge. In short, sales is made up of price multiplied by quantity.

Of course, money from sales is not the money to be pocketed by the company – there are costs that need to be taken into account. So, the next two items on the income statement represent different types of cost. The first of these is the cost of goods sold (COGS) or cost of sale (COS, which usually relates to services instead of goods). COGS/COS is then subtracted from the sales results in the gross profit/gross margin value. Clearly, gross profit/gross margin is not the ultimate profit the company makes because there is a second category of cost that must be taken into account: selling, general and administrative expenses (SG&A), which is also called *operating expenses* (OPEX). Deducting SG&A/OPEX from gross profit/gross margin leads to EBITDA, which stands for *earnings before interest, taxes, depreciation and amortisation*.

Let's stop for a moment to take stock. People sometimes treat COGS/COS as variable costs and SG&A/OPEX as fixed costs. While this is

		Acronym	
	Revenue/sales/turnover		£50,000
-	Cost of goods sold/cost of sales	COGS/COS	£32,000
	Gross profit/gross margin		*£18,000*
-	Selling, general and administrative expenses/ operating expenses	SG&A/OPEX	£6,000
	Earnings before interest, taxes, depreciation and amortisation	**EBITDA**	**£12,000**
-	Depreciation		£1,800
-	Amortisation		£2,000
	Earnings before interest and taxes	**EBIT**	**£8,200**
-	Interest		£2,500
	Earnings before taxes	EBT	*£5,700*
-	Taxes (at 40%)		£2,280
	Net income/net profit/net earnings		**£3,420**
-	Dividends		£342
	Retained earnings		£3,078

Figure 1.1 Sample income statement

technically not wrong, it may lead to confusion. Take, for instance, a 1-year employee contract. Should it be considered a variable or a fixed cost? Instead of thinking in these terms, a more pragmatic approach is to view COGS/COS as the direct costs of the inputs that are going into the goods and services that the business sells. Car seats and the wages of the labour force putting the cars together are examples of COGS. Salaries paid to lawyers in law firms are an example of COS.

SG&A/OPEX should be treated as indirect costs, i.e. costs that are not directly related to the inputs of the products or services that the company is selling. Examples of SG&A include the salaries of receptionists, the human resources team, the CEO and the marketing team. In other words, SG&A/OPEX are costs that are related to running the company or operation as a whole and are not specific to the actual goods and services sold.

EBITDA

EBITDA is a term often shrouded in mystery. This should not be the case. In fact, the concept behind it is pretty simple: showing how much a company has made after factoring in all of the costs – both direct and indirect – related to a company's *operational* activities, EBITDA therefore effectively represents how much a company has generated from its operations alone. By looking at the EBITDA, managers can quickly get a ballpark figure of its "operating profit". This is the main reason why, in corporate finance, EBITDA is one of the most popular ways to measure a company's performance.

However, newcomers to accounting and corporate finance often confuse the concept of EBITDA with EBIT (*earnings before interest and taxes*). This is not least because, in accounting, EBIT is seen as the "operating profit" of a business. In other words, we have two definitions for "operating profit" – one for accounting and the other one for corporate finance!

So, how does it work? Let's unpack the terms first. The difference between EBITDA and EBIT is depreciation ("D") and amortisation ("A"). Depreciation is applied to *tangible assets* (those items that we can touch, such as machines, equipment or a factory we bought in order to run our business), and amortisation relates to *intangible assets* (those things that we cannot touch but that are necessary to operate the business, like a brand or intellectual property rights).

In accounting, EBIT is considered "operating profit" because accountants treat depreciation and amortisation as a cost, which is *not* the case in corporate finance. In fact, depreciation and amortisation do not really exist in the book of finance. We will revisit this essential distinction in Chapter 3. For now, to make it easier to understand the rationale behind an income statement, let's assume depreciation and amortisation are absent (i.e. EBITDA is equal to EBIT).

How the money made from operations is distributed

From EBIT onwards, the income statement describes how the profit made is distributed. *Interest, taxes* and *net income/net profit/net earnings* represent how the company's gains are split among three main groups: interest to lenders, taxes to the government and, finally, net income/net profit/net earnings to shareholders. There are two important points that need to be highlighted here. First, while these three groups are entitled to receive the gains from the company, only two of them are investors, i.e. those who are putting money into the company with the hope of getting a return: lenders and shareholders. The government, on the other hand, is only "taking" and technically cannot be an investor. If the state buys a company's shares, it becomes a shareholder; if it lends money to the company, it becomes a lender. Even if it is providing a subsidy, it is still not an investor because it is not expecting a return. So, all in all, only lenders and shareholders are considered investors.

Second, the order in which the three parties are paid matters: lenders get paid first, then the government and, finally, the shareholders. Such an order of distributing profit has a couple of implications. First, interest on borrowing is paid out before taxes. This effectively means the company is getting tax benefits from borrowing (more on this in Chapter 5). Second, since the shareholders are the last to be paid, they face the most risk. Why? Imagine you are the last in the queue for tickets for a very popular show: there is a good chance that they will be sold out before you reach the counter. The same is true here. If money is first paid to others, whoever is the last to receive it has the highest probability of not getting his or her money. Since the shareholders are facing the highest risk, they must be getting the highest return. We will delve deeper into the relationship between risk and return in the next few chapters.

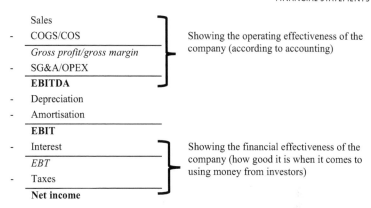

Figure 1.2 The income statement can be viewed as two main parts

By now it should be clear that the income statement is effectively made up of two parts, as depicted in Figure 1.2: one showing how good the company is at running the operations (*above* EBITDA (taking the corporate finance view) and EBIT (taking the accounting view)) and the other showing how good the company is at managing its finances or its financial effectiveness (*below* EBIT).

Beyond (beneath) net income

The income statement, however, does not stop at net income. Whereas lenders get their reward in the form of interest, and the government in taxes, shareholders can receive theirs in two ways. Shareholders – part owners of a company – usually get the return on their investments as 1) dividends, i.e. rewards the company can choose to pay out, usually on a regular basis, and 2) capital gains (selling a share at a price higher than it had been bought). Returning to the income statement in Figure 1.1, the first line under net income is dividends, which is one of the two ways for shareholders to obtain their return. Earnings that are not paid out in dividends are retained by the company – hence called retained earnings – for further investment instead. Retained earnings are related to capital gains, the latter of which means shareholders are making money by selling their shares at a price higher than the purchase price as the value of the shares goes up. But how? This brings us to the next financial statement: the balance sheet.

BALANCE SHEET

The balance sheet summarises what assets a company uses to create wealth and how these assets are financed at a specific point in time – for example, the 31st of December of a given year. In comparison, the income statement shows what activities have taken place over a specific period. A simple balance sheet is displayed in Figure 1.3. First, it is necessary to clear up a common misunderstanding. It is often said that assets on the left-hand side are "what you own" and liabilities and shareholders' equity on the other is "what you owe". This is arguably a poor depiction, not least because "own" carries a positive connotation and "owe" a negative one. When putting a positive and a negative idea next to each other, they compensate, but seldom balance.

What the balance sheet really says

A more coherent way to view the relationship between the two sides is this: the assets on the left-hand side are the means that the company can use to make money and the items on the right-hand side show how these means are funded. Let's start with the left-hand side. There are two main types of assets: current and fixed. Current assets are the means of production that the company owns up to 1 year before they disappear/ are used up. The common items found in current assets include cash, inventory and accounts receivable. Fixed assets, on the other hand, are those that last for more than a year. These assets can be both tangible and intangible. But, regardless of whether they are current or fixed assets, all of them share one thing in common: they are factors of production that the company owns for the purpose of producing and selling goods and services to make money.

The right-hand side of the balance sheet shows how these short- and long-term factors of production have been financed. This side

Assets		Liabilities and shareholders' equity	
Current assets (cash, accounts receivable and inventory)	£9,000	Current liabilities (short-term debt and accounts payable)	£6,000
Fixed assets	£25,000	Long-term debt	£8,000
		Shareholders' equity	£20,000
		Total liabilities and	
Total assets	£34,000	shareholders' equity	£34,000

Figure 1.3 Sample balance sheet

therefore tells us who has invested money and how much. Businesses can resort to both short-term financing (as shown in current liabilities, including short-term debt of up to 1 year and accounts payable) and long-term debt and equity (i.e. financing/funding/capital that supports the company for more than 1 year).

Breaking down the balance sheet in this way shows that it is not about what the company owns or owes. Total assets are more about "what production factors I have got to make money", and the total liabilities and shareholders' equity are about "how I am financing the production factors that I have got".

Going back to the earlier discussion on the connection between retained earnings and share price, any money left over after dividends are paid (as shown on the income statement) would be earnings retained by the company for future investments. Since this is still money belonging to the shareholders, the leftover is added to the shareholders' equity. In the example shown in Figure 1.4, the company made retained earnings of £3,078 (drawn from Figure 1.1, the income statement), which would then go into shareholders' equity, increasing this line from £20,000 to £23,078 and the total liabilities and shareholders' equity from £34,000 to £37,078.

Since a balance sheet has to balance, this means that the total assets also have to go up to £37,078. The question now is which of the assets – current or fixed – would go up by £3,078? The answer is fixed assets. Even though this will be explained in greater detail in the next chapters, it is key to understand at this stage that the company should be able to make more money through investing the £3,078 wisely in fixed assets. The value of the company will go up as a result because it is expected to make more money in the future. With each share being entitled to more gains in the future, the value of each share would increase. It must be noted that share prices are not only relevant to large, publicly traded companies. This is not the case at

Assets		Liabilities and shareholders' equity	
Current assets (cash, accounts receivable and inventory)	£9,000	Current liabilities (short-term debt and accounts payable)	£6,000
Fixed assets	£25,000 + £3,078	Long-term debt	£8,000
		Shareholders' equity	£20,000 + £3,708
		Total liabilities and	
Total assets	£37,078	shareholders' equity	£37,078

Figure 1.4 Retained earnings to the balance sheet

all – the same concept applies to businesses of all sizes. Before looking at this in depth, it is necessary to spend a little bit of time covering the last type of financial statement – the cash flow statement.

CASH FLOW STATEMENT

The cash flow statement describes how cash is generated and used within a company. Since this statement plays much less of a role in corporate finance than the first two, we are going to keep the discussion brief. Whereas the income statement is concerned with profit, the cash flow statement deals with cash. And cash and profit *are* different. Why? How? Consider this: Bob sells a product to a buyer. However, the buyer does not have to pay Bob until 60 days from now. In this case, even though he has sold the product and made a profit, he is not pocketing the actual cash for another 60 days. He would have to ensure that he has enough cash to pay for things – say, electricity to run the business – during this time period.

This illustrates an important point in financial management: even if Bob's business is very profitable, if it has only very little cash, it may not be able to pay for electricity to keep going, in which case it will have no alternative but to shut down despite its profitability. Almost all activities conducted by a business require cash – to buy raw materials, to pay salaries, to service the interest on bank loans, to buy or rent equipment and plants, etc. In this sense, managing cash properly is more important than merely shooting for profitability, at least in the short run. Chapter 3 will look at profit versus cash in detail.

As shown in Figure 1.5, the cash flow statement has four main parts. The "operating cash flow" is the cash generated by the company's own operations. It is calculated by first adding back the depreciation and amortisation to the profit made from the company. Next to be included is the cash that the company can generate from three main items of working capital – accounts receivable, inventory and accounts payable, all of which will be discussed in detail in Chapter 4.

The second part includes the cash generated *and* used from a business's investing activities, i.e. the "investing cash flow". If the company is buying equipment, the company has to use cash to pay

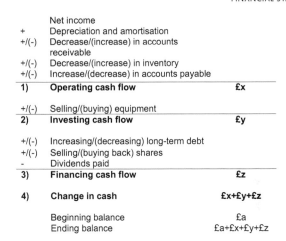

	Net income	
+	Depreciation and amortisation	
+/(-)	Decrease/(increase) in accounts receivable	
+/(-)	Decrease/(increase) in inventory	
+/(-)	Increase/(decrease) in accounts payable	
1)	**Operating cash flow**	**£x**
+/(-)	Selling/(buying) equipment	
2)	**Investing cash flow**	**£y**
+/(-)	Increasing/(decreasing) long-term debt	
+/(-)	Selling/(buying back) shares	
-	Dividends paid	
3)	**Financing cash flow**	**£z**
4)	**Change in cash**	**£x+£y+£z**
	Beginning balance	£a
	Ending balance	£a+£x+£y+£z

Figure 1.5 Sample cash flow statement

for it and, therefore, ends up having less cash. Cash flows are, in this case, used for investing activities and the amount goes down. Likewise, if the business is selling any of its equipment or building, it gets cash in return. Hence, the investing cash flow goes up.

The third part is about the "financing cash flow". This is related to raising financing externally, either by borrowing or selling more shares. Any time the company takes out a new loan or sells shares of the company, it immediately adds more cash to its coffer. If it decides to pay its debt down or off, or to buy back some shares from the current owners, then the company needs to spend some cash.

The fourth and final part simply tallies up the amount of cash generated and used, together with the current amount of cash owned by the company. Once we add up the cash flows generated and used through these three activities ($£x + £y + £z$) in a specific year, we know how the cash position of the business – how much cash it has – has changed that year. Subsequently, by adding this change in cash to the amount of cash that the company had at the start of the year (beginning balance of $£a$), we can obtain the total amount of cash – called the *ending balance* – which reflects the amount that the company has at its disposal for the year. This amount ($£a + £x + £y + £z$) then goes into the "cash" line under current assets on the balance sheet, which is the money that the business can use to invest in its operations and investments.

SUMMARY

This chapter has looked at the three accounting statements as a starting point to corporate finance. The income statement shows how much money is made from selling the goods and services that the company produces, after subtracting all the costs, and shows how the money made is distributed first to the lenders (in the form of interest), then the government (taxes) and, finally, the shareholders (dividends and share price increase). The balance sheet describes, on the left-hand side, how much and what kind of short- and long-term means of production a company has and, on the right-hand side, how these means of production are financed by debt and equity. Whereas the income statement shows how profit is made and the balance sheet demonstrates with what the profit is made, the cash flow statement describes how the cash is generated and used to pay various expenses so that profit can be made.

There is one main question that remains unanswered: how should the retained earnings – the £3,078 mentioned on p. 11 – be invested in order to raise the share price? This, in essence, is what corporate finance is about. The next chapter therefore looks at how companies can make the right investments.

FINANCIAL DECISIONS AND INVESTMENT CRITERIA

CHAPTER OVERVIEW

This chapter starts by defining what corporate finance is. It then moves to its central subject: making good investments. A good investment takes place when a person/company gains more from a project/opportunity than what has been put in in the first place. This chapter discusses the three most popular investment criteria and tools for assessing projects – net present value, payback and internal rate of return.

WHAT IS CORPORATE FINANCE?

Imagine you are running a company. No matter the type of business, you will have to answer the following three important questions if it is to succeed economically:

1   What kind of investments should you undertake in order to grow the company and make economic gains? Put differently, if your business requires you to buy buildings, equipment and machinery now, how can you know whether you would be able to recuperate these purchases *in the years to come*? Alternatively, if you are in a research and development (R&D) intensive business – such as software or pharmaceuticals – how can you tell if you will be able to recover and make an earning exceeding the costs of the R&D activities?
2   How do you raise the money needed to finance the investments, projects and opportunities selected? Do you borrow or do you accept new co-owners?

3   Have you got enough money to deal with day-to-day business activities? Are you collecting money from customers fast enough? Are you paying suppliers prematurely?

Corporate finance helps us answer these questions and guides us to make better financial decisions. Let's look into these questions in more detail. The first question is a matter of *capital budgeting*. As the name suggests, it is about allocating capital – a limited resource – wisely. If a company has unlimited funding, it could (in theory) pursue any potentially money-making investment opportunities. In reality, very few (if any) companies have such a luxury. Good investments mostly involve buying value-creating means of production, which often come in the form of fixed assets. Hence, capital budgeting is directly related to fixed assets on the balance sheet, shown in (1) of Figure 2.1. With only a limited amount of money at their disposal, businesses must choose their investments carefully, selecting only those opportunities and projects that can create value. In the rest of this chapter, three tools are introduced to help managers with this selection.

Identifying a good investment opportunity is one matter, financing it is another. How companies can finance their investments depends on their *capital structure*. The capital structure refers to the split of a company's two main forms of capital – *long-term debt (borrowing)* and *shareholders' equity*. This mix is shown in (2) in Figure 2.1. Since both

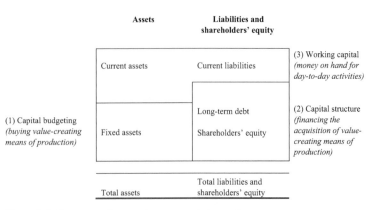

Figure 2.1 Corporate finance shown on a balance sheet

means of financing have their pros and cons, choosing which to use and how much to raise is an important consideration for managers. We will look at this topic in depth in Chapters 5 and 6.

The last question relates to *working capital*, which refers to the money needed to run a business on a day-to-day basis. Any business needs sufficient cash on hand to pay bills and meet unexpected expenses. Working capital is calculated by subtracting the current liabilities from the current assets, which is directly related to (3) in Figure 2.1. A more detailed discussion on the exact nature of working capital is presented in Chapter 4.

Looking at capital budgeting, capital structure and working capital, we can see that corporate finance is about thinking about and looking into the *future* – creating economic gains in the future from investment decisions that we are making today. By contrast, accounting describes what has already happened. It describes and documents the business and financial activities that happened in the *past*.

CAPITAL BUDGETING

So far, this chapter has mentioned investments multiple times. But what exactly is an investment? Here is the simple definition that is going to be used throughout this book: an investment is an opportunity, such as a project, that offers the investor the potential to get more money in return compared to what has been put in. Put differently, an investment potentially creates an output that is greater than the input.

Even though this is the definition of investment for this book, in truth, investors always want to maximise the gains as much as possible. Consider three investment opportunities, all of which will guarantee gains in return. If Charlie has enough capital to invest in all three of these opportunities, she should. However, if she only has capital for one of them, she would want to get the most out of the scarce capital that she puts in: she wants to get the most out of it. In other words, she wants to maximise the return that she can get from her investment by choosing out of the three the one that gives her the most return. Hence, it is important to know how to assess individual potential investment opportunities.

Imagine that you are presented with the possibility of investing in a silver mine. There are two important questions to consider: 1) how much can you make from selling the silver and 2) how much should you invest in the extraction process in order to achieve a gain? If the amount you stand to profit from the silver mine is greater than what you invest in it – meaning the output is greater than the input – then this is a good investment.

Continuing with this example: having consulted an expert, you learn that there is a 10-year reserve of silver in the mine. By the end of the 10th year, the mine will have no silver left and therefore will produce no value for you. You also find out that, for every year of extraction after all the costs have been taken into account, you stand to make £300,000. After some research, you also find out that the initial investment you need to kick-start the mining process is £1m.

It should be a simple exercise to figure out if it is a good investment. All you should have to do is add up £300,000 for each of the 10 years, minus the £1m of the initial investment, and you would know the amount of gain you can expect to pocket. So, £300,000 a year × 10 years − £1m = £2m is what you will make altogether, right? Well, not quite. This is because there is a need to account for the time value of money.

The time value of money and present value

The best way to explain the *time value of money* is through an example. Imagine you are given two choices:

1 Receiving £1,000 today or
2 Receiving £1,000 in a year from now

Ignoring inflation, which of the two options would you pick? Your answer would most likely be the first. The reason is that you get to spend the windfall immediately. Yet, even if you are not spending it now, you should still select the first option because you can invest it straight away. So, if you take the £1,000 now and put it in a bank account that pays, say, 5 per cent interest, in 1 year's time, you will have £1,050 in the account. This is more than the second option of receiving £1,000 in a year's time. In other words, the sooner you have the money in your pocket, the sooner you can make money from it. This is the logic behind the time value of money, which means that money is worth more today than tomorrow (by the same logic, money is worth less and less further away in the future).

Going back to the silver mine example, it is therefore incorrect to simply add up the £300,000 over a 10-year period. This is because the £300,000 received in the 2nd year of operation is worth less than the £300,000 received in the 1st year in today's terms. To figure out how much this 10-year stream of money is worth today, we need to perform an operation called *discounting*.

Let's use an example to understand the concept of discounting. Charlie is depositing £100 in a bank account today, which pays 10 per cent interest every year. So, how much money would she have in the account a year from now? The answer is £110 (interest = £100 × 10% = £10, plus the original £100 deposit). And how much would Charlie have the following year? The amount would be £121 (interest = £110 × 10% = £11, plus the £110 already in the account). Table 2.1 summarises these calculations and shows their mathematical representation.

In this example, £100 today is worth £110 in 1 year and £121 in 2 years. Discounting involves reversing this logic by saying that £121 in 2 years' time is worth £100 today. By the same definition, £110 in 1 year's time is worth £100 today. The statement sounds exceedingly simple, yet it encapsulates the foundation of (corporate) finance; we can now figure out what any future amount of money is worth today. Mathematically, discounting over 2 years can be represented by Equation 2.1.

$$\frac{£121}{\left(1+10\%\right)^2} = £100 \tag{2.1}$$

Table 2.1 Interest calculation

	Year 0 (today)	Year 1 (next year)	Year 2 (the year after next)
Conceptual representation	£100	Interest: £10 (£100 × 10%)	Interest: £11 (£110 × 10%)
		Account balance: £100	Account balance: £110
		Total: £110	Total: £121
Mathematical representation	£100	£100 × (1 + 10%) = £110	£100 × (1 + 10%) × (1 + 10%) = £121
			which is the same as
			£100 × (1 + 10%)^2 = £121

In this case, £121 discounted by 10 per cent for 2 years is £100, with the exponent of "2" in the equation denoting the number of years discounted. The "10 per cent" is called the *discount rate*. The answer showing today's value (£100) is called the *present value* or simply PV.

With these ideas in place, we can return to the silver mine. As we mentioned, it is incorrect to add up the £300,000 received in each of the next 10 years to estimate the stream of gains from extracting the silver. The appropriate approach that takes the time value of money into consideration is to discount all the amounts to be received. The calculation is shown in Equation 2.2.

$$
\begin{aligned}
&\frac{£300,000}{(1+10\%)} + \frac{£300,000}{(1+10\%)^2} + \frac{£300,000}{(1+10\%)^3} + \frac{£300,000}{(1+10\%)^4} \\
&+ \frac{£300,000}{(1+10\%)^5} + \frac{£300,000}{(1+10\%)^6} + \frac{£300,000}{(1+10\%)^7} + \frac{£300,000}{(1+10\%)^8} \quad (2.2) \\
&+ \frac{£300,000}{(1+10\%)^9} + \frac{£300,000}{(1+10\%)^{10}} = £1,843,370
\end{aligned}
$$

The PV of the silver mine project is £1,843,370. Effectively, this is what this project generates in the next 10 years in today's terms.

Discount rate and risk

Consider another situation. Suppose Bob buys a machine with which he can produce goods that allow him to make £500,000 next year. The machine itself costs £450,000. Is it a good investment if the discount rate is 5 per cent? The PV calculation is shown in Equation 2.3.

$$
PV = \frac{£500,000}{(1+5\%)} = £476,190 \quad (2.3)
$$

Since the gain of £476,190 is bigger than the cost of £450,000, it is a good investment opportunity. But what happens if you are not so sure whether the gain next year would amount to £500,000? In other words, what if there is some *risk* involved? In this case, to account for the higher risk involved, Bob would increase the discount rate. But why?

To answer this question, consider that someone whom you do not know – say, a certain Terry – asks you to lend him £10,000 for a year.

He is offering to pay 2 per cent interest. In all likelihood, you would not lend to him because you can fairly easily collect 2 per cent interest simply by putting your £10,000 in a bank, with the additional benefit that it is a lot easier to get your money back from the bank than from Terry and is thus safer. In effect, it is a lot riskier to lend money to him.

Now, let's say Terry is willing to pay 12 per cent interest instead. Regardless of whether you are happy to lend or not at this rate, you would feel more comfortable and more inclined to do so than in the situation where he is offering you a pitiful 2 per cent. The (somewhat) higher reward compensates for the risk of loaning to him. From this, it is possible to glean an important insight as an investor: you would charge the borrower a higher interest rate if you perceived that a specific investment carried a high level of risk. Essentially, this means that you will demand a higher return.

The same principle can be applied in the earlier example with Bob. If he perceives that investing in the purchase of the machine carries a higher risk, he will ask for a higher return to compensate for the greater perceived risk. So, for example, he may choose to use 11 per cent, instead of 5 per cent, as the discount rate.

As shown in Equation 2.4, with a discount rate of 11 per cent, the PV is £450,450. This PV with an 11 per cent discount rate is *smaller* than the PV with a 5 per cent discount rate (£476,190) because the gain you can *expect* to make is *lower* when the risk is *higher*.

$$PV = \frac{£500,000}{\left(1+11\%\right)} = £450,450 \tag{2.4}$$

Discount rate and the cost of capital

At this point of the discussion, some readers will be keen to have answers to the following question: what exactly is the discount rate? To answer this, let's say you are happy to sign off the loan to Terry with a 15 per cent interest rate. When you do that, you are effectively asking for a 15 per cent return on this investment. Now, put yourself in Terry's shoes for a minute. What does the *same* 15 per cent represent to him? It is the cost he has to bear for accessing the £10,000 that you are lending him. This leads to an important point, which is shown in Table 2.2: the cost that Terry has to pay for using your money is what you are expecting to get as the return.

Table 2.2 Cost and return on the loan to Terry

The 15 per cent interest rate is . . .	
. . . from Terry's perspective	*. . . from your perspective*
The cost that Terry has to pay for having access to your money	The return that you need from lending Terry the money

Table 2.3 Cost of using capital and return on the capital provided

The discount rate is . . .	
. . . from the company's perspective	*. . . from the investors' perspective*
The cost of using the capital provided by the investors	The return needed by the investors who are providing the capital

More generically speaking, when a company needs access to capital, it has to pay for the use of this capital. The *cost of capital* for the company represents the return that the capital provider (the investor) needs given the perceived risk. This is summarised in Table 2.3.

Hence, the return that the investors seek and the cost for the company to use the capital are directly related – so much so that they are essentially two sides of the same coin. So, the discount rate is the cost of capital for the party accessing the capital, which is also the return needed by the investors.

This conclusion also provides the first clue to another question that some readers may have: how is the discount rate determined? The answer depends on whether it is debt and equity financing that the company is using and how much return the providers of this capital demand. This will be explored in greater depth in Chapters 5 and 6. But, for now, let's continue with the discussion on capital budgeting.

INVESTMENT DECISION-MAKING CRITERIA

There are three main criteria that managers can use when assessing an investment – net present value, payback and internal rate of return. They are discussed in turn.

Net present value

So far, the PVs calculated are only showing how much a gain in the future is worth today. The PVs in Equations 2.3 and 2.4 are not the amount of money made. In both cases, Bob has to buy the £450,000 machine before being able to make the £500,000 in the year that follows. So, taking the example with the 5 per cent discount rate, the actual amount that Bob gains is the difference between the gains in today's terms and the initial investment, i.e. £476,190 − £450,000 = £26,190. This £26,190 realised − the amount of money that goes into Bob's pocket − is the result of making an investment using the *net present value* (or NPV) method.

NPV is a way of determining whether or not it is worth going ahead with a project. Think about it: Bob would probably only invest £450,000 to buy a machine if he is confident that this investment is going to earn him more than what he spent on the machine. In contrast, he will forget about the investment if what he thinks he will make (in today's value) will not even cover the cost of the machine. This is why:

> If NPV is *greater* than 0, the project should be accepted; if NPV is equal to or smaller than 0, the project should be rejected.

Revisiting the earlier silver mine example, you are not pocketing the PV of £1,843,370, as calculated in Equation 2.2, if you are going ahead with exploiting the mine − you have to make an initial invest-ment of £1m up front. Therefore, your NPV, or the value created, is £1,843,370 − £1,000,000 = £843,370.

Bringing it all together, the formula for calculating NPV is shown in Equation 2.5, where C_0 denotes the initial amount needed to be spent, C_t the gain made in each of the years and r the cost of capital.

$$NPV = \left(C_0\right) + \frac{C_1}{(1+r)} + \frac{C_2}{(1+r)^2} + \frac{C_3}{(1+r)^3} + \cdots \qquad (2.5)$$

In practice, NPV is the most popular method used to assess the cost-effectiveness of investment opportunities.

Payback

NPV is not the only tool for making investment decisions. There are other contenders. One of them is *payback*. It refers to how long it will take to recover the initial investment. For instance, a manager at a manufacturing plant is considering buying a new component worth £20,000. By using it to replace the old one, the company can run the machine more efficiently – so much so that it can generate a saving of £20,000 within 2 years. If the manager is happy with a payback period of 2 years, then she should accept this project. If the payback time is too long to be acceptable, the manager should not buy the component. Put differently, as long as the upfront investment can be recovered within the acceptable payback period as determined by the decision-maker, the project should go ahead. If not, it should be rejected.

The payback method is simple and intuitive to use. After all, this investment criterion looks at how quickly you can get your money back. While payback is easy to use, it is not without its pitfalls. First, unlike NPV, it ignores the time value of money. Second, just focusing on how long it will take to recover the initial outlay is effectively saying that all the values beyond the payback period are irrelevant to the business decision. In other words, this method is biased towards short-term gains. Projects that only produce value later in the future are put at a disadvantage when using the payback method. Third, it is a very subjective method, given that the decision to accept or reject a project depends heavily on some arbitrary cut-off points set by the decision-makers. It is because of these shortcomings that companies tend to use this method only for small and less important investments.

Internal rate of return

A much more potent competitor of NPV is *internal rate of return* (or IRR). It is easier to explain this method by first showing how IRR is calculated. This involves three steps:

1 Take the formula to calculate NPV (like in Equation 2.5). Next, turn NPV into 0.
2 Replace all of the r values with "IRR". The changes in these two steps are reflected in Equation 2.6, where C_0 again represents the

upfront investment required to kick-start the project and C_t is the gain made in each of the years.

$$0 = \left(C_0\right) + \frac{C_1}{(1+IRR)} + \frac{C_2}{(1+IRR)^2} + \frac{C_3}{(1+IRR)^3} + \cdots \qquad (2.6)$$

3   Solve for IRR.

Whereas with the NPV method an investment should be accepted when NPV > 0, in the case of IRR, a project should be accepted as long as IRR is *larger* than *r*. Why? Consider the silver mine example and apply these three steps. Equation 2.7 shows the setup for calculating the IRR.

$$\left(\pounds1,000,000\right) + \frac{\pounds300,000}{(1+IRR)} + \frac{\pounds300,000}{(1+IRR)^2} + \frac{\pounds300,000}{(1+IRR)^3}$$
$$+ \cdots + \frac{\pounds300,000}{(1+IRR)^{10}} = 0 \qquad (2.7)$$

The resulting IRR would be 27 per cent. This is also the maximum discount rate that the investment can take before it stops creating value – anything greater than 27 per cent would lead to a negative result. Therefore, as long as the cost of capital is lower than this maximum rate, the project would create value. In this example, since the IRR of 27 per cent is greater than the discount rate of 10 per cent, this silver mine project should be accepted.

A major advantage of IRR is that, as long as a manager knows the cost of capital of her company, she can make a meaningful comparison between the cost of capital and IRR in order to make an investment decision. For example, if your company's cost of capital is 12 per cent, and you identify that a potential new project has an IRR of 18 per cent, you can immediately know that this project will create value.

A common practice for some investment companies – such as venture capital firms – is to use an IRR of 30 per cent as the benchmark. At the same time, they promise a 20 per cent return to their own investors. This effectively means their cost of capital is 20 per cent. Therefore, when they find an investment opportunity that has an IRR of 30 per cent or above, these investment companies can be confident that such an opportunity would be value-creating.

The IRR method is superior to payback because it is more in line with the NPV method. Nevertheless, finance professionals tend to prefer to use NPV because it indicates the gains in value terms – showing how much value is created – from an investment. Furthermore, it offers the advantage of easy comparisons between two or more projects. All it takes is to look at which one of them has the higher NPV to find out which one creates the most value.

SUMMARY

Making the right investments lies at the heart of corporate finance. Businesses need to be able to choose and pursue value-creating investment opportunities (capital budgeting), raise the financing to support the investment opportunities identified (capital structure) and ensure there is enough money available to be tied up to keep the operations going in order to capture the full value from the investment opportunities (working capital). This chapter has focused on capital budgeting, the basis of which is the time value of money. This refers to the fact that gains that are further into the future are worth less in today's terms. The main implication is that, in order to meaningfully compare the gains to be received from a project with the initial outlay of the project, it is necessary to convert all the future gains into today's value, i.e. calculate the PV. To do so, all the money to be received in the future is discounted using the discount rate/cost of capital.

Three common methods for making investment decisions have been presented. The most popular is NPV. In this case, if NPV > 0 – i.e. all the money to be gained in the future from the project (in today's value) is larger than the amount of money needed to get it started – then this project is acceptable. An alternative to NPV is payback. While payback is easy to use, it can oversimplify complex investments, potentially leading to wrong decisions. IRR, on the other hand, is more rigorous. A project is said to be acceptable when IRR is greater than the cost of capital (IRR > r). So, as long as a company's cost of capital is smaller than the IRR of a given project, the project can be accepted.

One major element that has not received much acknowledgment in this chapter is how to come up with C – the "gains" and "money" made from investments/projects/opportunities. This requires a separate discussion, which is the focus of the next chapter.

APPENDIX: HOW TO DISCOUNT Cs THAT GO ON FOREVER

Regardless of the investment decision methods, we have been assuming that the number of years of Cs is finite. But what would happen if they were to go on forever?

Top-prize lottery winners face the following dilemma: should I take all the winnings in one go now or receive it as individual small amounts that last until the day I die? How can I compare the two options? To answer this question, we need to figure out the PV for the latter choice. This can be achieved through the concept of perpetuity.

Perpetuity

Perpetuity assumes that all future gains remain the same – i.e. $C_1 = C_2 = C_3 = C_4$, with all of the everlasting Cs being exactly the same in value. This is shown in Equation A2.1.

$$PV = \frac{C_1}{(1+r)} + \frac{C_2}{(1+r)^2} + \frac{C_3}{(1+r)^3} + goes\ on\ forever\ and\ ever \quad (A2.1)$$

Skipping the mathematics behind it, the concept of perpetuity dictates that this is equal to C_1 divided by the discount rate, as represented in Equation A2.2.

$$PV = \frac{C_1}{r} \quad (A2.2)$$

Let's illustrate its application through an example. If a university wants to set up a scholarship that pays £2,000 annually forever, how much money would be required at the outset? If the bank pays an interest rate of 4 per cent on the deposit (as shown in Equation A2.3), it will need £50,000 to create a yearly payout of £2,000.

$$PV = \frac{£2,000}{4\%} = £50,000 \quad (A2.3)$$

Look at this another way: if the university always has a balance of £50,000 in the bank, it will be able to generate £2,000 of interest every year forever (assuming the interest rate remains at 4 per cent forever).

Growing perpetuity

As the name suggests, growing perpetuity is akin to perpetuity, with the difference that the gain grows at the same rate (g, as in growth rate) every year. This means that C_2 is C_1 that has grown by the rate of g and, subsequently, C_3 is C_2 that has grown by the rate of g. Said differently, C is growing by a constant rate forever. The formula for calculating an investment with such a constantly increasing payout is shown in Equation A2.4.

$$PV = \frac{C_1}{r - g} \tag{A2.4}$$

Using the earlier scholarship example, the university wants to create a scholarship that does not just pay out £2,000 a year, but also catches up with the 3 per cent inflation every year. Again, receiving a 2 per cent interest rate (as displayed in Equation A2.5), the university will have to establish a pool of £200,000 to meet its need.

$$PV = \frac{£2,000}{4\% - 3\%} = £200,000 \tag{A2.5}$$

FREE CASH FLOWS

CHAPTER OVERVIEW

The goal of this chapter is to examine the "gains" that can be realised from projects and investment opportunities. Specifically, this involves defining and using the concept of *free cash flows* (FCF). The chapter starts with a comparison of profit and cash, underscoring their differences. It then focuses on the three main components of FCF. At the end of this chapter, various observations on FCF estimations are made.

MEASURING VALUE

The previous chapter has explained that value can be created by investing in projects that have a positive net present value (where NPV is greater than 0). Equation 3.1 is a repetition of Equation 2.5.

$$NPV = \left(C_0\right) + \frac{C_1}{(1+r)} + \frac{C_2}{(1+r)^2} + \frac{C_3}{(1+r)^3} + \cdots \tag{3.1}$$

However, the discussion has so far centred around how to *create* value; little has been mentioned about how to *measure* value – that is, how the annual gains/benefits (the Cs in the equation) are estimated. Understanding what these Cs involve matters because they can significantly affect the outcome of NPV.

The peril of profit

So, how do you estimate the gains/benefits? The knee-jerk reaction answer is "profit". Seemingly, this makes sense. After all, as stated in

Chapter 1, profit – which is called the *bottom line* – is what companies make from selling the goods and services after all the costs have been taken into account. So, in order to decide whether an investment is worth pursuing, it would seem right to discount the annual profits that can be made over the number of years in NPV calculations.

Well, not quite. While it is true that profit is the leftover gain after all the costs have been deducted, profit represents the gains to only one of the two groups of investors: the shareholders. You may recall that in Chapter 1 we explained that the income statement shows how effective a company's operations are and to whom the money made from the operations is distributed. Even though there are three groups of recipients (debtholders being the first to be paid, then the government and then shareholders last), there are only two groups of investors – debtholders and shareholders. In other words, any gains or benefits made by a company should go on to reward *all* investors. The problem with profit is that it is the reward to the shareholders only. It is thus necessary to find a measure of value for all investors.

Cash, on the other hand, is a better measure of value. Before investigating cash further, it is necessary to first examine the difference between profit and cash. To illustrate this, let's look at a highly simplified situation of two companies in Figure 3.1.

Company A is far more profitable than company B: company A is already profitable in January, whereas company B is still making a loss of £1,000 in March. This is because A has a much lower cost of goods sold (COGS) than B. It would seem that company A is doing much better than company B.

Yet, the cash situation of the two companies tells a very different story. Whereas company A is using up an increasing amount of cash as the months go by (by March it has to raise £58,000 in cash from somewhere as its balance is negative), company B faces the opposite, accumulating more and more cash over time (with £96,000 in cash by March). How could this happen? Why would a profitable company have only little cash in hand while a loss-making business accumulates cash?

The answer lies in the time difference in how the two companies receive money from their customers and pay their suppliers. Company A pays suppliers before receiving payments from customers. By contrast, company B receives payments from customers immediately and pays suppliers later. In the process, while A is depleting its cash, B

COMPANY A: Has profit but no cash

Income statement

Assumptions
COGS as % of revenue: 65%
Depreciation, amortisation, interest, taxes: 0

	January	February	March
Revenue	£ 40,000	£ 50,000	£ 60,000
COGS	26,000	32,500	39,000
Gross profit	14,000	17,500	21,000
SG&A	10,000	10,000	10,000
EBITDA	4,000	7,500	11,000
Depreciation	-	-	-
Amortisation	-	-	-
EBIT	4,000	7,500	11,000
Interest	-	-	-
EBT	4,000	7,500	11,000
Tax	-	-	-
Net income	£ 4,000	£ 7,500	£ 11,000

Cash situation

Assumptions
Cash position in January £ 10,000
Accounts receivable 60 days
Accounts payable 30 days

	January	February	March
Cash at the start of the month	£ 10,000	£ -	£ (36,000)
Inflow			
Paid by customers	-	-	20,000
Total inflow	-	-	20,000
Outflow			
Pay suppliers	-	(26,000)	(32,500)
Pay expenses	(10,000)	(10,000)	(10,000)
Total outflow	(10,000)	(36,000)	(42,500)
Cash at the end of the month	£ -	£ (36,000)	£ (58,500)

COMPANY B: No profit but has cash

Income statement

Assumptions
COGS as % of revenue: 85%
Depreciation, amortisation, interest, taxes: 0

	January	February	March
Revenue	£ 40,000	£ 50,000	£ 60,000
COGS	34,000	42,500	51,000
Gross profit	6,000	7,500	9,000
SG&A	10,000	10,000	10,000
EBITDA	(4,000)	(2,500)	(1,000)
Depreciation	-	-	-
Amortisation	-	-	-
EBIT	(4,000)	(2,500)	(1,000)
Interest	-	-	-
EBT	(4,000)	(2,500)	(1,000)
Tax	-	-	-
Net income	£ (4,000)	£ (2,500)	£ (1,000)

Cash situation

Assumptions
Cash position in January £ 10,000
Accounts receivable Immediately
Accounts payable 60 days

	January	February	March
Cash at the start of the month	£ 10,000	£ 40,000	£ 80,000
Inflow			
Paid by customers	40,000	50,000	60,000
Total inflow	40,000	50,000	60,000
Outflow			
Pay suppliers	-	-	(34,000)
Pay expenses	(10,000)	(10,000)	(10,000)
Total outflow	(10,000)	(10,000)	(44,000)
Cash at the end of the month	£ 40,000	£ 80,000	£ 96,000

Note: Brackets denote that it is a spending/an outflow of money

Figure 3.1 Profit versus cash

is building up the amount of cash held. This is the essence of working capital management, the topic of the next chapter.

But, for now, the most important insight to be gained from this comparison of companies A and B is that, as time goes by, even though A is more profitable, it will run out of cash very soon. The consequence is that it will have no money to pay utilities and rent, which could lead the business to cease trading immediately. On the contrary, despite the fact that company B is still suffering losses, it would have enough cash to give itself a chance to make the business profitable. Granted, if losses continue to mount over time, it will eventually have to shut down. But, for the moment at least, it has enough cash to ensure its survival for the short run, while company A is not in a position to do so.

Cash is king

It should be clear now that cash is essential to the survival, running and growth of a business. Yet, there is a larger practical problem with profit: you cannot pay for things with it. Imagine there are two pots, one filled with cash and the other profit. With the cash pot, you can count exactly how much physical money there is. Moreover, with it, you can run your business – for instance, using it to pay bills and salaries and wages to staff, to buy raw materials from suppliers, or to build new facilities. Vendors would only accept cash. You have to pay wages and salaries to employees in the form of cash. (Even if you are paying them with stock options, they would only accept them if they knew they could sell them for cash.)

By contrast, you cannot do much with the profit pot. Indeed, all profit is showing is how much has been made for the shareholders and not much else. This is the reason why people always say "cash is king".

All of these reasons make cash a much better measure of value. The question now is how to estimate the amount of cash to be gained from a project in the future. The natural response to this question is to turn to the cash flow statement, introduced in Chapter 1. Yet, this view is wrong for a simple reason. Accounting documents like cash flow statements are looking backwards at what has already happened. Since they are a recording of the *past*, one can/should know exactly when and how much cash has been generated or used. It is no coincidence that accounting – to account for something – also means to reason why something exists or happens.

When assessing an investment opportunity of which the gains are only emerging in the *future*, we estimate the future stream of cash – better known as *cash flows* – that a project/opportunity would produce. This is where we turn to one of the most, if not *the* most, important concepts of corporate finance: FCF.

THE MAKEUP OF FCF

FCF are made up of three components: 1) cash flow from operations, 2) capital expenditure and 3) change in net working capital.

1) Cash flow from operations

The first component is called *cash flow from operations* (CFO, or *operating cash flow*). It describes the amount of cash generated from the project/opportunity through operations. The formula to calculate CFO is shown in Equation 3.2.

$$\text{Cash flow from operations}\left(CFO\right) = \text{Net operating} \atop \text{profit after tax} + \text{Depreciation} + \text{Amortisation} \tag{3.2}$$

We can break this formula into two parts: a) net operating profit after tax (NOPAT) and b) depreciation + amortisation.

a) NOPAT: Admittedly, the term NOPAT just creates more confusion as it is yet another concept revolving around the operating profits. We can get some clarity by looking at its calculation, as in Equation 3.3.

$$\begin{aligned} NOPAT &= EBIT \times (1 - tax\ rate) \\ &= (EBIT \times 1) - (EBIT \times tax\ rate) \\ &= EBIT - taxes\ paid\ to\ the\ government \end{aligned} \tag{3.3}$$

In Chapter 1, we explained that earnings before interest and taxes (EBIT) represents the amount of money a company has made, which is distributable to debtholders and shareholders, as well as used to pay taxes. Looking at NOPAT through this lens, NOPAT is the profit generated through operations that is left after taxes have been paid. It therefore represents the amount of money that can be distributed to shareholders and debtholders.

b) Depreciation + amortisation: The next step to calculating CFO is to add depreciation and amortisation together. But what is the rationale behind this? The answer lies mainly in the fact that depreciation and amortisation are accounting concepts but do not reflect "real" outflows of cash. To understand the relationship, we need to turn to the second component of FCF.

2) Capital expenditure

The second item is called *capital expenditure*, or more simply CAPEX. CAPEX can be thought of as purchases that are large and one-off or infrequent. To illustrate how CAPEX is related to depreciation and amortisation, consider the following situation in terms of how a purchase is counted: Charlie acquires a £20,000 van and pays for it in full to run a transport service between two towns. The van is expected to have a life of 5 years, after which it will be worth nothing.

In finance, as the purchase is a one-time, unique event, it is counted as CAPEX. As shown in Table 3.1, the spending of £20,000 is recorded in year 0 (now). This is because Charlie pays the entire sum of the van immediately.

This is for finance. Accounting, on the other hand, is different. It does not record items differently from finance: any newly acquired assets are depreciated or amortised over time. Depending on the number of years that the assets can last, the purchase price is spread over the same time horizon. So, for Charlie, the van will depreciate at £4,000 a year (£20,000 ÷ 5 years = £4,000). So, in accounting, the van purchase will be recorded as shown in Table 3.2.

Table 3.1 Recording the van purchase in finance (as CAPEX)

	0	1	2	3	4	5
CAPEX	(£20,000)					

Note: Brackets denote that it is spending/an outflow of money.

Table 3.2 Recording the van purchase in accounting (as depreciation) in the income statement

	0	1	2	3	4	5
Depreciation		(£5,000)	(£5,000)	(£5,000)	(£5,000)	(£5,000)

Note: Brackets denote that it is spending/an outflow of money.

As a reminder, depreciation is for tangible assets like Charlie's van, whereas amortisation is for intangible assets. Even though there is no amortisation involved here, the same idea applies if intangible assets are present.

Several important insights can be gained here. First, the reason why depreciation and amortisation must be added to NOPAT to calculate CFO is because, if we do not do so, we will be double-counting the purchase. How? Let's assume that, from the shuttle service offered, Charlie makes an earnings before interest, taxes, depreciation and amortisation (EBITDA) of £6,000 every year for the next 5 years. As shown in Figure 3.2, to calculate EBIT, £4,000 in depreciation would have to be deducted from EBITDA. With EBIT, we can then proceed to calculate CFO. This is first done through EBIT $\times$ (1 − tax rate) to attain NOPAT, which equates to £1,400 every year.

What happens if depreciation is *not* added to NOPAT? The cost of buying the van will be recorded twice – once under "depreciation" and once under "CAPEX" (see situation 1 in Figure 3.2).

By adding *back* the depreciation, as demonstrated in situation 2, we can avoid the double-counting problem. In this situation, the van purchase is only considered under "CAPEX", which is the correct way of calculating cash flows because this is the amount of money spent at the outset of this shuttle-service project.

Another insight to be gained here is why depreciation and amortisation are often called *non-cash items*. The cash Charlie used towards the purchase of the van was spent in year 0 and not paid out over 5 years. Depreciation and amortisation are mere accounting concepts with no cash involved.

This also explains a mystery highlighted in Chapter 1: why "operating profit" in accounting is EBIT and in finance is EBITDA. The answer, as it turns out, is simple: in accounting, any big, infrequent purchase is broken up to be depreciated or amortised, which, in turn, is counted as part of the operations. Accounting reasons that

Situation 1: Not adding back D&A (wrong)

	0	1	2	3	4	5
	£	£	£	£	£	£
EBITDA		6,000	6,000	6,000	6,000	6,000
Depreciation (and no amortisation)		(4,000)	(4,000)	(4,000)	(4,000)	(4,000)
EBIT		£ 2,000	£ 2,000	£ 2,000	£ 2,000	£ 2,000
Tax rate = 30%						
NOPAT [= EBIT × (1-tax rate)]		£ 1,400	1,400	1,400	1,400	1,400
Depreciation		-	-	-	-	-
CFO		£ 1,400	£ 1,400	1,400	1,400	1,400
CAPEX	(£20,000)					

The business is counted twice – the first time under "depreciation" and then the second time under "CAPEX".

Situation 2: Adding back D&A (correct)

	0	1	2	3	4	5
	£	£	£	£	£	£
EBITDA		6,000	6,000	6,000	6,000	6,000
Depreciation (and no amortisation)		(4,000)	(4,000)	(4,000)	(4,000)	(4,000)
EBIT		£ 2,000	£ 2,000	£ 2,000	£ 2,000	£ 2,000
Tax rate = 30%						
NOPAT [= EBIT × (1-tax rate)]		£ 1,400	1,400	1,400	1,400	1,400
Depreciation		4,000	4,000	4,000	4,000	4,000
CFO		£ 5,400	5,400	5,400	5,400	5,400
CAPEX	(£20,000)					

No "double-counting" problem because what's counted under "depreciation" in the first place is being "uncounted" – added back after NOPAT is calculated. This leaves the bus purchase to be recorded under CAPEX only.

Note: Brackets denote that it is a spending/an outflow of money

Figure 3.2 (Avoiding) double-counting the purchase in the FCF calculation

a proportion of any big purchase is "used up" every year; hence its value goes down (it depreciates or amortises) over time, as the asset gradually loses its effectiveness and value. In finance, the concepts of depreciation and amortisation simply do not exist.

3) Change in net working capital

The third component of FCF is the change in *net working capital* (NWC). The next chapter will examine the subject of NWC in greater depth, but for now, it is sufficient to understand that NWC refers to the money that is needed for the day-to-day operations of a business. To illustrate how this component of FCF works, consider the situation shown in Figure 3.3.

Imagine that we want to manufacture and sell one widget. At the start of the process, we need to buy the raw materials. Let's say we can buy from supplier A for £10 all that is needed to produce one widget, for which we pay in full immediately. For the next 10 days, our business makes a widget. After that, the widget produced sits in the warehouse for a further 22 days before our customer buys it for £45. Assuming that the only cost to us is the £10 in raw materials, the profit to us is £35. There is no doubt, therefore, that this is a lucrative activity.

However, this handsome profit can only materialise if our business can survive "out of pocket" of £10 for 32 days – 10 days of production and 22 days until the sale. Eventually, we recover the £10 when we have sold the widget. The fact that £10 is tied up throughout the 32-day period illustrates the concept of NWC. As for the *change*,

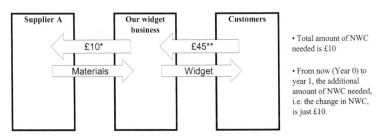

Assume production time to be 10 days, and that there are 22 days before the widget is sold
* NWC, which is the money that is tied up until the widget is sold
** With the widget sold, the NWC is recovered

Figure 3.3 Change in net working capital (year 1)

since we start with no NWC before the production of the first widget, we need to have £10 to be tied up in the operations to make the profit 32 days later. So, the change in NWC in this case is £10.

Let's see what happens in year 2 when we produce not just one but two widgets. Figure 3.4 shows the situation in year 2, with the 2nd year activities marked in dotted lines. To source the materials, we again buy from supplier A and immediately pay for £20 worth of raw materials, which is enough for producing two widgets. Our business is now able to manufacture two widgets in 10 days. It also manages to sell them both 22 days after they are made. With the selling price remaining at £45 each, our business would make a profit of £70 (£35 × 2 widgets) out of £20 of costs! The catch here, however, is this: even though we are making more profit than before, the cash situation has actually come under more pressure; instead of having only £10 tied up in the operations, like in year 1, the total NWC has amounted to £20 in year 2. This underscores an important reality of business: the more a company sells, the more money will be tied up and, hence, the more NWC will be needed.

Whereas the total amount needed is £20, the *change* in NWC is only £10. This is because we only have to inject an *extra* £10 in cash to be tied up this year. In other words, rather than the full amount of NWC, we are only concerned with the change – the difference – from one year to another when calculating the FCF generated, as we want to know how much *additional* money we need to tie up in order to keep the business activity going.

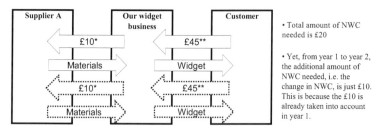

Assume production time to be 10 days, and that there are 22 days before the widget is sold
Dotted line denotes Year 2 activities
* NWC, which is the money that is tied up until the widget is sold
** With the widget sold, the NWC is recovered

Figure 3.4 Change in net working capital (year 2)

Table 3.3 Change in net working capital (years 1 and 2)

	0	1	2	3
Total NWC	£–	£10	£20	£–
Change in NWC	(£10)	(£10)	£20	–

Note: From year 0 to year 1, the additional NWC is £10. For year 2, even though the total NWC is £20, the additional NWC on top of what was required in year 1 is also £10.

Since there is no NWC needed for year 3 as the operation has ceased, all the outstanding NWC (of £20) will be fully recovered.

Brackets denote that it is a spending/an outflow of money.

There is one more point about the change in NWC. Let's say that, after we have sold the two widgets in year 2, we decide to shut down the business for good. What would happen to the NWC? The answer is that we would get all of it back. Why? Because, from the moment we sold the two widgets, we recovered the £20 that was tied up. At the same time, since we are not going to build any more widgets, we have no need to buy materials from supplier A and, therefore, no money is tied up. What this means is that, when a project comes to an end, the entire outstanding amount of money tied up will be recovered in full. This is called *working capital recovery*. The calculation of the change in NWC is summarised in Table 3.3.

FCF

Putting the three components together, we can now calculate the FCF in each year of a project/investment opportunity. This is summarised in Figure 3.5.

A key concern when looking at the three FCF components is to determine whether the cash is flowing in (inflows) or out (outflows). This is perhaps best illustrated with an imaginary briefcase, as shown in Figure 3.6. For instance, spending money on CAPEX is an outflow because it requires taking money out of the briefcase. On the other hand, proceeds from selling old assets are counted as inflows, as the cash received goes into the briefcase. Drawing from the widget example earlier, the £10 for each year that is tied up in operations requires taking money out of the briefcase (outflow). By contrast, the money from having sold the widget is going into the briefcase (inflow).

	1. CFO
+	2. CAPEX
+	3. Change in NWC
=	**FCF**

Figure 3.5 FCF calculation

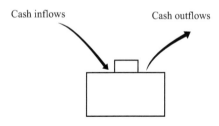

Figure 3.6 Cash inflows and outflows

Now that the components of FCF have been covered, what does FCF tell us? Imagine that you are holding the briefcase in your hands on the 31st of December of a given year. Inside, you will find a pile of cash that is the end amount that has come from your receiving (inflows) and drawing down to spend (outflows) throughout the year. So, what do you do with this leftover amount? The answer: it could be used to pay interest and/or pay down the debt, both of which represent the returns to the debtholders. Alternatively, the money could go towards paying dividends to shareholders or back into the business for further investments – the latter of which, if used properly, would boost the share price. It is out of these observations that FCF represents a measure of the value created: the money that is *free* from any business obligations, which can be *freely* distributed to all the investors. In other words, FCF represent the value created for all capital providers, including both the debtholders and shareholders of a company for each time period.

This is the reason why we can replace the Cs with FCF in the NPV calculation, as shown in Equation 3.4.

$$NPV = \left(FCF_0\right) + \frac{FCF_1}{(1+r)} + \frac{FCF_2}{(1+r)^2} + \frac{FCF_3}{(1+r)^3} + \cdots \qquad (3.4)$$

A mathematical illustration of FCF and NPV is shown in the appendix at the end of this chapter.

CONSIDERATIONS WHEN ESTIMATING FCF

There are four considerations that have to be taken into account when calculating FCF, which help to determine what should or should not be counted as cash flows.

Relevant cash flows only

It is important to keep in mind that only those cash flows that would emerge as a result of the project taking place – relevant cash flows – should be counted. To illustrate this point, imagine your company makes FCF of £100 every year forever, as shown in Table 3.4. Now you are assessing an investment opportunity that would allow you to make £10 in FCF a year for the next 5 years, with an initial outlay of £30 today. To properly assess whether this project should be undertaken, the £10 FCF received in the next 5 years and the initial investment of £30 should be included in the calculation. The £100 in FCF that your company is making every year is irrelevant to the project. After all, the company has the stream of £100 in FCF a year with or without the new project actually taking place.

Erosion and synergy

While our example may sound simple, in reality, things can be less clear-cut. Consider a software company that is looking to introduce a new version of software to replace the current one. In this case, it must take into account both the revenue gained from the new version *and* the revenue lost from the current edition. So, when Microsoft launched Windows 10, it not only had to count the FCF earned from this new operating system, but it also had to take into

Table 3.4 Relevant cash flows only

	0	1	2	3	4	5	6	7 …
Current ongoing FCF	–	£100	£100	£100	£100	£100	£100	£100
FCF from new project	(£30)	£10	£10	£10	£10	£10	–	–

Note: Brackets denote that it is a spending/an outflow of money.

consideration the FCF lost from ceasing to sell Windows 8. The fact that the introduction of a cash-providing project can cannibalise the sale that could otherwise be made is called *erosion*.

In other situations, there could be *synergy*. For example, let's take a small airline that currently serves a single route from Aachen, Germany, to Bergen, Norway. The company is now considering adding a new route from Bergen to London, UK. When estimating the FCF that can be made from this new route, the airline not only takes into account the number of passengers that can be expected to fly on this new route, but it also considers the potential additional passengers flying via Bergen on an Aachen–London journey.

Sunk costs

Another key consideration when looking at what to count as part of the FCF calculation is the so-called *sunk cost*. A concept taken from economics, this refers to a cost that has already been incurred and therefore should have no bearing at all on our investment decisions. To illustrate it, let's say your watch has stopped working. You go to a watch specialist, to whom you pay £60 to open it up and look at it.

Days later, you receive a call from the specialist, informing you that the repair would cost £300. Should you go ahead with the repair? You may say you would rather sell the broken watch or use the £300 to buy a new one instead. These are all valid propositions. What you must *not* do, however, is follow this line of logic: "I have spent £60 on having the watch opened and checked, so I may as well spend £300 to have it fixed". This is wrong. Why? Because the £60 is already spent. Whether you are getting the watch repaired or not, you are not going to be able to recover the £60. Looking at it another way, the decision to spend the £300 is an independent decision. The £60 in this case is said to be a sunk cost, as it should not affect your decision to repair the watch or not.

Now consider another situation. A business is considering a property development project. It decided to spend £15,000 on a report to assess the current market demand. As tempting as it is to include this £15,000 as part of the expenditure in the FCF calculation, it is a sunk cost: the £15,000 is already spent, whether or not the development project is going ahead. For this reason, this should be excluded from the FCF calculation.

Allocated costs

Last but not least, when estimating FCF, it is important to allocate the costs accordingly. Let's say a hospital is considering adding a new wing to its existing building. Its management is considering assigning 15 per cent of the existing personnel to run the new wing. However, it should not include the cost of the 15 per cent of staff in the FCF calculation. Why? Because this 15 per cent of current employees are already part of the hospital's operating costs. They are already hired, with or without the new wing being built. The cost of the 15 per cent of staff should therefore be excluded in the calculation of FCF.

SUMMARY

Whereas the previous chapter examined how to create value through NPV, payback and internal rate of return, this chapter has focused on measuring value creation through FCF. FCF represents all the value gained from an investment opportunity, which, in turn, can be given to all the investors as returns to the capital that they have provided to finance the company's operations. FCF has three components – CFO, CAPEX and change in NWC. Lastly, the chapter has also presented several factors that must be considered when estimating FCF in general.

Given that NWC plays a crucial role in value creation, the next chapter discusses this oft-neglected (but vitally important) topic.

APPENDIX: PULLING IT ALL TOGETHER IN AN EXAMPLE – MC PRODUCTION, INC.

MC Production, Inc. is currently examining a 5-year project that is expected to generate sales of £100,000 in the 1st year of operation, with a 5 per cent increase in each of the 5 years that follow. The COGS and selling, general and administrative expenses (SG&A) of this investment opportunity in year 1 are £40,000 and £15,000, respectively. Whereas COGS is expected to go up by an annual rate of 3 per cent, SG&A will go up by 2 per cent every year. The tax rate is 30 per cent. The initial outlay in the equipment is £160,000. There is no amortisation. NWC is estimated to be 20 per cent of the annual sales. MC Production's cost of capital is 10 per cent (see A) in Figure 3.1A.

A) Assumptions

Revenue in year 1	£	100,000
Growth in sales in each subsequent year		5%
COGS in year 1	£	40,000
Growth in COGS in each subsequent year		3%
SG&A in year 1	£	15,000
Growth in SG&A in each subsequent year		2%
Tax rate		30%
Equipment (to be purchased in year 0)	£	160,000
Depreciation method	Straight-line	
Length of the project	5 years	
NWC as a percentage of revenues next year		20%
Cost of capital		10%

B) Income Statement

	0	1	2	3	4	5
Revenue	£	100,000	105,000	110,250	115,763	121,551
COGS		(40,000)	(41,200)	(42,436)	(43,709)	(45,020)
Gross profit		60,000	63,800	67,814	72,053	76,530
SG&A		(15,000)	(15,300)	(15,606)	(15,918)	(16,236)
EBITDA		45,000	48,500	52,208	56,135	60,294
Depreciation		(32,000)	(32,000)	(32,000)	(32,000)	(32,000)
EBIT	£	13,000	16,500	20,208	24,135	28,294

C) Free Cash Flows Calculation

	0	1	2	3	4	5
1) CFO						
NOPAT	£	9,100	11,550	14,146	16,895	19,806
Depreciation		32,000	32,000	32,000	32,000	32,000
CFO	£	41,100	43,550	46,146	48,895	51,806
2) CAPEX						
+ CAPEX	£ (160,000)					
3) NWC						
NWC	20,000	21,000	22,050	23,153	24,310	
+ Change in NWC	£ (20,000)	(1,000)	(1,050)	(1,103)	(1,158)	£ 24,310
FCF	£ (180,000)	£ 40,100	£ 42,500	45,043	£ 47,737	£ 76,116
Discounted FCF	(180,000)	36,455	35,124	33,842	32,605	47,262
NPV	£ 5,287					
IRR	11.03%					

Note: Brackets denote that it is a spending/an outflow of money

Annotations:

- CAPEX divided by the length of the project
- Obtained by the EBIT in each year multiplied by (1 - tax rate)
- In year 0, the company has to put in £20,000 of NWC, which is 20% of year 1 revenues. Given that it is a cash outflow, it would be -£20,000. Calculation-wise, this is obtained by subtracting £20,000 from £0.
- This is a cash inflow because this is where the company recovers all the outstanding NWC.
- This shows that an extra £1,000 will be tied up by the activity. To calculate this, minus £21,000 from £20,000.

Figure 3.1A MC Production's project

In order to figure out if this project should be accepted or not, the company uses both the NPV and IRR investment criteria. Either way, it has to calculate the FCF. Based on our earlier assumptions, MC Production first produces the income statement to obtain the EBIT (see B) in Figure 3.1A).

CFO

Once the company has estimated the EBIT in each of the years for the entire project, it can proceed to calculate NOPAT. To estimate the amount of depreciation, it assumes a straight-line method – i.e. the equipment loses an equal amount of value every year. Hence, the annual depreciation is £160,000 divided by 5 years, or £32,000. Obtaining the CFO is only a matter of adding NOPAT to the depreciation.

CAPEX

Since MC Production only invests £160,000 today with no further investment throughout the project, the only CAPEX in this case is £160,000 in year 0.

NWC

In this project, NWC is assumed to be 20 per cent of the annual sales. The complication here, however, is the change in NWC. Let's take a look at the change in NWC in year 0, which is (£20,000). Where does this come from? This comes from the fact that the NWC required in year 1 is £20,000. But why is it shown in year 0? This is because this is the amount that MC Production will have to inject into the project before the operation starts to generate sales. Think of the raw materials and inventory that the company would need to purchase and hold before turning them into sellable products. Explained another way, starting with no money tied up in operations, MC Production would have to put cash into the operation to get the business activity going, ending with £20,000 tied up by the end of year 0.

Now, let's look at what happens in year 1. In this year, the company can expect to have £21,000 tied up as NWC altogether. However, since it already has £20,000 tied up, MC Production only needs to put in an extra £1,000 to be tied up to finance the NWC. The result is that the change in NWC for year 1 is £1,000.

The change in NWC is calculated for each of the years throughout the project. In the last year, the outstanding amount of NWC (£24,310) will be recovered in its entirety. This is because no more cash will be tied up with the project having come to an end.

FCF and conclusions

Adding up the CFO, CAPEX and the change in NWC in each of the years from 0 to 5, MC Production can estimate the annual FCF that this project could be making. The next step is to discount these FCF with the cost of capital of 10 per cent to take into account the idea of the time value of money.

By adding up all the discounted FCF, MC Production reaches an NPV of £5,287. Since this is larger than 0, it means that the project is value-creating and should be accepted. At the same time, the IRR is 11.03 per cent. As this is larger than the 10 per cent cost of capital, the same conclusion can be reached: that this project is worth undertaking as it generates value for the company.

As can be seen in this example, the resulting NPV heavily depends on the assumptions that drive the different components of FCF. While the calculation of FCF, with enough practice, is neither particularly difficult nor complicated to perform, obtaining the right assumptions is what managers should be spending their time and energy on. Very often, this is a difficult task that requires a good amount of work. Yet, it is of paramount importance if the goal of the investment assessment is to figure out if the project is able to create value. As the saying "rubbish in, rubbish out" goes, no matter how robust a financial model or projection may look, using unrealistic assumptions will only lead to unrealistic analyses and results.

NET WORKING CAPITAL MANAGEMENT

CHAPTER OVERVIEW

The importance of managing net working capital (NWC) or working capital cannot be over-emphasised (the terms refer to the same thing and are, in general, used interchangeably). Many tend to think that only finance directors and treasurers need to understand how working capital works, but that would be wrong. Understanding how it can be properly managed is essential to the economic survival of any business. Companies have to make sure that they have enough cash in hand to keep the day-to-day activities going. As illustrated in Figure 3.1 in the previous chapter, a business – like company A – that is running out of cash is edging ever closer to failure. This chapter goes through the calculation of NWC, proceeds with a discussion on its effective management and finishes with a review of its implications.

HOW NWC IS CALCULATED

Let's look closer at how NWC works. NWC describes the difference between current assets and current liabilities. Therefore, NWC is calculated by subtracting current liabilities from current assets, as shown in Equation 4.1.

$$NWC = Current\ assets - Current\ liabilities \tag{4.1}$$

Current assets

To see the rationale behind this formula, let's unpack these two balance sheet items. As discussed in Chapter 1, current assets are those items that the company owns up to 1 year before they disappear/are used up. The most common current asset items are shown in Table 4.1.

While cash and inventory are both self-explanatory, accounts receivable may require a bit more explaining. Imagine the following situation: Bob is a nail manufacturer and has sold to you, a DIY retailer, a box of nails for £100. Bob has already delivered the box of nails to you. There are two things that can happen here regarding payment: either you pay Bob the £100 now, or you pay later.

In the latter case, if both parties agree to paying later – say, 60 days – then the £100 would become the accounts receivable to Bob; he is waiting to *receive* the money that you have committed to pay 60 days from now.

Current liabilities

Current liabilities, on the other hand, are what the company has to pay up within 1 year. The most common items in current liabilities are listed in Table 4.2.

Table 4.1 Most common items in current assets

Items	Explanation
Cash	Money previously earned by the company that is not used (it is sitting in a bank account)
Inventory	Goods and products that are sitting in a warehouse waiting to be sold (therefore, companies that sell services – such as consulting firms – do not have inventory)
Accounts receivable	The amount of money that a company is waiting to *receive* (i.e. for its clients/customers to pay up) after delivering goods or services to them

Table 4.2 Most common items in current liabilities

Items	Explanation
Short-term debt	Loans that have been taken out, which have to be paid back within a year
Accounts payable	Outstanding amounts that a company *pays* to a seller, having already obtained the goods or services ordered

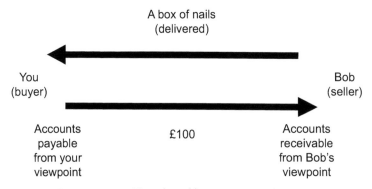

Figure 4.1 Accounts receivable and payable

Whereas the nature of short-term debt is rather obvious, that of accounts payable may be less so. Returning to the earlier illustration with Bob, the nail manufacturer, you are only going to pay £100 to him 60 days from now, even though you have already received your box of nails. As mentioned, for Bob, the £100 you owe him is accounts receivable. But, from your perspective, the same £100 represents accounts payable: an amount of money that you are going to *pay* him. The relationship is summarised in Figure 4.1.

IMPLICATIONS OF NWC

Now, here is the interesting part: for Bob, there is no difference in terms of profit whether you pay now or later – he has sold the box of nails for £100 (with the total cost to him being smaller than this amount) and has made a profit out of it. Where it does have an impact, however, is his cash position. Let's investigate this further. Despite the fact that he has sold the box of nails to you, it will only be paid for 60 days from now. Effectively, Bob is £100 out of pocket for the next 60 days. So, if, say, Bob is required to pay £60 in extra tax immediately, he would not be able to use the £100 from the sale to you to settle this bill, because you are still holding onto the money. If he does not have the money, he will have to borrow £60 from – and pay interest to – a bank to sort this out.

It should now be clear that, even though Bob appears to be in the good position of someone who has made a sale and is owed money, the reality is that he has less cash at his disposal. This example highlights two important points. First, as discussed before, there is a huge difference between profit and cash. Concluding a sale does not automatically bring in cash immediately. It all depends on the payment terms.

Second, the more boxes of nails Bob sells, the greater his receivables will be and the more cash will be tied up. If Bob allows the receivables to grow unchecked, he will eventually run out of cash and get into a financial predicament. He will have to be able to manage this soon to avoid cash problems. For instance, if, next year, Bob were to sell you 10 boxes of nails instead of 1 box (assuming the costs of production are still smaller), he will increase his sales and profit tenfold. The flip side, however, is that he will have £1,000 of cash tied up for 60 days! It must be noted that the same idea also applies to inventory. Just like accounts receivable, the more a business builds up its inventory, the more money gets tied up.

You, on the other hand, are likely to fare much better. By being able to keep Bob's £100 – or £1,000 – for 60 days, you have more cash at your disposal, which you can use for different purposes such as paying bills or collecting interest if you put it in the bank – all financed by the "zero-interest loan", courtesy of Bob. So, even though it may not sound good that you owe others money, you are actually better off in terms of cash availability, as you can use the money temporarily provided by others.

MANAGING NWC

This discussion shows that it is essential for a business to understand the concept of working capital and how to manage it. How can you manage NWC in your favour? To answer this question, let's simplify Equation 4.1 by excluding cash from current assets and short-term debt from current liabilities, reaching what is shown in Equation 4.2.[1]

$$NWC = \text{Current assets (without cash)} - \text{Current liabilities} \\ \text{(without short-term debt)} = \text{Accounts receivable} + \\ \text{Inventory} - \text{Accounts payable} \qquad (4.2)$$

Now, imagine you are running a wholesale business. Four main activities are generally involved in running such a business. In a logical order (as shown in Figure 4.2), these are i) buying goods from

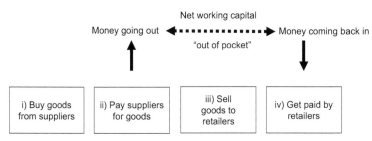

Figure 4.2 A breakdown of NWC (part 1)

suppliers, ii) paying these suppliers, iii) selling the goods to retailers and iv) getting paid by the retailers. In this process, you will see money flowing out of your business when you pay the suppliers. Later on, when you receive money from your customers (the retailers) for the goods they have bought from you, you will see money flowing back into the company. Effectively, the time period and amount of money between these two time points – money flowing out and money coming in – is when you are "out of pocket" (i.e. when money is tied up in the business operations). Also called the *cash conversion cycle*, this "out of pocket" period is the working capital that you have to inject to run this wholesale business.

This means that, if you want to have as little cash tied up as possible, you will have to shorten the time period when you are out of pocket and minimise the amount. But before going through how this can be achieved, let's see how the actions are related, as illustrated in Figure 4.3.

1   Between iii) selling to retailers and iv) collecting money from them is accounts receivable;
2   Between i) buying and iii) selling goods is inventory; and
3   Between i) buying goods from suppliers and ii) paying for them is accounts payable.

As can be seen in the figure, to calculate your NWC in this example, it is simply 1) accounts receivable + 2) inventory − 3) accounts payable, which exactly matches Equation 4.2 earlier in this section! But the key point of Figure 4.3 is that it offers a view on how to

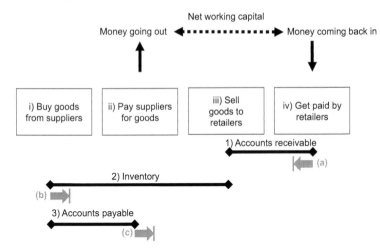

Figure 4.3 A breakdown of NWC (part 2)

reduce NWC. To lower the cash required to run this business (the dotted line between money going in and going out), you can:

• *Decrease accounts receivable* by reducing the amount of accounts receivable extended to customers and/or shorten the period that they have to pay up (shown by arrow (a));
• *Decrease inventory* by carrying a smaller inventory and/or selling it more quickly (shown by arrow (b)); and/or
• *Increase accounts payable* by stretching your suppliers and negotiate for a larger accounts payable and/or longer period to pay up (shown by arrow (c)).

Each of these actions would allow you to lower the working capital required/cash tied up in the company operations.

MANAGING NWC IN DAYS

In reality, it is common practice to manage NWC in days. Let's return to the earlier example of the transaction between you and Bob, the nail manufacturer, in which you have to settle your £100 purchase in 60 days. From Bob's perspective, he will not be getting his accounts receivable for another 60 days.

However, to improve his working capital and lower the amount of cash tied up, Bob can shorten your payment period. If he manages to cut the accounts receivable from 60 to 45 days, he will obtain cash 15 days earlier (of course, from your perspective, you have 15 days fewer to take advantage of the £100 that is still in your hand). Similarly, businesses can manage their NWC by reducing inventory, such as by letting the goods sit in warehouses for a fewer number of days. It is better to have stock staying in warehouses for 10 days instead of 30, as less cash is tied up as a result. Alternatively, if firms can stretch their accounts payable for a longer time period – say, 30 to 40 days – they have access to extra cash for 10 days.

IMPLICATIONS OF MANAGING WORKING CAPITAL ON FREE CASH FLOWS (FCF)

Increasing the amount of financing

Managers can be unaware of the importance of working capital management. The result is that some businesses, especially start-ups, can run out of cash if too much of it has been tied up in their operations. Yet, certain companies are well positioned to do the opposite – take advantage of NWC to finance their business.

Take supermarkets as an example. Grocers frequently pay their suppliers in 60 days; simultaneously, they have almost no accounts receivable because shoppers pay immediately at the checkout. Many suppliers doing business with major supermarket chains do not have enough bargaining power to shorten their payment period. If chain grocers manage their inventory well, they are able to use the money they owe suppliers – accounts payable – to fund their business. The lesson here is clear: businesses can squeeze more cash out of their operations by managing their NWC through reducing accounts receivable, reducing inventory and increasing accounts payable.

Improving FCF

Lowering the NWC requirements can also improve FCF. The previous chapter showed that NWC is part of the FCF calculation. If companies can lessen the amount of cash being tied up in a project, they can see their FCF going up. The calculation is shown in

$$
\begin{array}{ll}
 & \text{1. CFO} \\
+ & \text{2. CAPEX} \\
+ & \underline{\text{3. Change in NWC }\downarrow} \\
= & \textbf{FCF }\uparrow
\end{array}
$$

Figure 4.4 Lower change in NWC, get more FCF

Figure 4.4. Recall that change in NWC describes how much additional NWC you need to inject in a particular time period. Now, if you can reduce this additional money needed, you will see more money left (i.e. FCF) in the briefcase for all your investors.

THE MISCONCEPTION OF NEGATIVE NWC

As a final comment to this chapter, let's look at what happens if NWC is negative. Negative NWC arises when current assets are lower than current liabilities. To many, this is considered "bad" because there are more liabilities than assets. Yet, as it should be clear by now, having more accounts payable (an item in current liabilities) is actually good for the cash position! By contrast, having too much in accounts receivable and inventory (both are items in current assets) ties up the use of money, which is bad for business. It is therefore important to recognise that a negative NWC is not necessarily bad. The actual makeup of the short-term assets and liabilities is more important when assessing the working capital situation of a company. Compare the following two situations:

Situation 1: Cash < Short-term debt
Situation 2: (Accounts receivable + inventory) < Accounts payable

Even though in both situations the working capital is negative (as current assets are smaller than current liabilities), situation 1 is not very favourable because a company with more short-term debt than cash may not have enough money to pay back this debt when it is due. Situation 2, on the other hand, can be a very good one: Just look at the supermarket chain example mentioned earlier. The conclusion here is that, depending on what the NWC is composed of, negative NWC is not necessarily bad. Many think that the presence of the term "negative", as in "negative NWC", represents a bad cash situation. This does not have to be the case. As the old expression goes, "The devil is in the detail".

SUMMARY

This chapter has delved into the issue of working capital management, showing its components and how it can be properly managed. The key is to lower the accounts receivable and inventory, as well as raising the accounts payable. It also mentions the advantages of managing NWC well and clears up two misconceptions.

Now that we have completed the discussion on the FCF part of the NPV concept, it is time to divert our attention to the *r* in the NPV formula, which refers to the cost of capital. In general, companies have access to two types of capital – debt and equity, which are discussed in turn in the next two chapters.

NOTE

1 Technically, the end result of this equation is called net *operating* working capital, but for the purpose of simplicity, such a distinction is not made here.

DEBT

CHAPTER OVERVIEW

In general, companies can resort to two major types of capital to finance their capital expenditure. They can sell shares, essentially giving part of the company away in exchange for capital injection into the business, or they can take on debt (i.e. borrow money). Debt is the focus of this chapter. With debt, in return for receiving an immediate loan, a company will typically make regular interest payments and pay back the borrowed sum when it is due. Since the lenders can expect to receive a predetermined amount on a regular basis, debt as a product is often called *fixed income*. This chapter examines the two most common forms of debt: bank loans and bonds. Subsequently, it discusses the concept of financial leverage and the implications for companies of using debt.

BANK LOANS

Bank loans as a financing possibility are easy to understand. Individuals and companies can walk into a bank and borrow a certain amount of money, promising to pay interest at an agreed time and frequency. They also promise to return the original loan when it is due. So, if a business takes out a bank loan of £10,000 for 1 year and the bank charges 7 per cent interest, 365 days from now the business must pay the bank both £700 (£10,000 × 7%) in interest and the £10,000 taken out in the first place. This is all rather simple.

However, here is a trickier question: is the lending bank an investor in the business? The answer is yes. You may recall that Chapter 1 explained that the income statement of any business shows that lenders, together with shareholders/owners, make up the two groups of investors. Why are lenders investors when they are not becoming a part-owner of the business? Because making an investment does not necessarily require ownership. We also discussed in Chapter 2 that an investment is an opportunity to potentially get more money back than what you put in in the first place. So, as long as the bank expects to receive more in return (both the interest collected and loan payback) than what it put in (the loan), it is making an investment. Understanding this allows us to clarify one of the most confusing yet important aspects of corporate finance: the relationship between the cost of using the capital provided and the return.

COST OF CAPITAL PROVIDED AND RETURN TO INVESTORS: TWO SIDES OF THE SAME COIN

Let's revisit the bank loan arrangement described earlier, this time considering the perspectives of both parties. This is shown in Table 5.1.

A company borrows £10,000 from the bank and has to pay £700 in interest. This £700 (or 7 per cent) interest is effectively the cost that it has to pay in order to access the £10,000 forwarded by the bank.

At the end of the lending period, the bank will have made £700 out of the £10,000 lent – that is a 7 per cent return on its investment. How does the bank decide that the interest should be 7 per cent and not less or more? When determining what return to ask for, the bank has to assess the risk of lending the money to this company. It only makes economic sense to provide the loan if the return is sufficiently large to cover the risk. The higher the risk of lending to the company, the higher the return the bank should demand. So, in this case, after making an assessment, 7 per cent is the minimum to justify the risk of lending. Yet, usually, the bank cannot charge more. Why? In an efficient banking system, if the bank charges more, a competing

Table 5.1 Two sides of the same coin (bank loan)

	From the company's viewpoint . . .	*From the investors' viewpoint . . .*
The interest rate is the . . .	Cost of using the bank loan	Return needed by the bank

bank can take away the business by offering only 7 per cent interest. Therefore, the interest rate that it charges is the return that it needs. In financial jargon, this is called the *required (rate of) return* for the bank.

Those studying corporate finance often think the cost of a company using a bank loan and the return the bank receives are two separate concepts; they are not. They are two sides of the same coin. The cost of bank loans and the required return by the bank are one and the same.

As can be seen later, this concept is also applicable to equity and another form of debt – bonds.

BONDS

While most people have a good idea of how a bank loan works, bonds can be a mystery to many. They are an instrument that most governments and major corporations around the world use to borrow money. A bond is an IOU ("I owe you") – that is, a note stating that we owe someone money. The note specifies how much we are paying and when. A highly simplified example of a bond is shown in Figure 5.1.

In this case, since we are the one issuing the IOU, we are actually selling the bond. This makes us a bond seller. Furthermore, as we are selling a promise of making multiple payments in the future in exchange for receiving money now, we are effectively borrowing money from whoever is willing to buy this bond from us. This means the holder, buyer and investor of this bond are basically the lending parties. Table 5.2 summarises and clarifies this relationship further.

IOU	
	2018
We, CFTB PLC, promise to pay the holder of this bond 10% of the amount below in	2019
each of the years in the period between 2018 and 2021.	2020
We also promise to pay £100 at the end of 2021.	2021

Figure 5.1 A highly simplified example of a bond

Table 5.2 Who's who in bonds

As we are borrowing money using the bond, we are the . . .	*The party that is accepting this bond is the . . .*
Borrower	Lender
Bond issuer	Bond investor/bondholder
Bond seller	Bond buyer

Basic makeup of a typical bond

As shown in Figure 5.2, there are several key features of a bond.

Coupons are essentially the annual interest we (the borrower) have to pay the bondholders who lent us money. So, in this example, to get paid in 2018, the lender would tear out the coupon along the dotted lines for that year and send it to us. Upon receiving the coupon, we would send a cheque for payment. The lender repeats this action every year for the following 3 years until the last coupon is sent.[1]

But how big is the coupon payment? The answer lies in the *coupon rate*. In this example, the coupon rate is 10 per cent. The payment to the lender is therefore 10 per cent of the face value of £100 (or £10) a year. There are two important points to remember here. First, the coupon rate serves only one function: to determine the size of the coupon. It has no other purpose. Second, even though the coupon is akin to interest, the term "interest" is rarely (if ever) used in association with bonds. The right terms are "coupons" and "coupon rate".

Face value denotes the amount that we will pay bondholders when the bond reaches the end of its life (in this example, in 2021). To

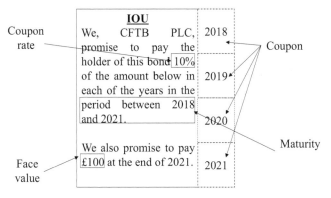

Figure 5.2 A highly simplified example of a bond and its key features

put it in perspective, face value can be thought of as the amount of money that we return to the lenders.

Maturity refers to the period of time before the bond expires – that is, the number of years before the IOU comes to an end, by which time all of the coupons would have been claimed and the face value paid. In our example, the maturity is 4 years.

Calculation of bonds

In the discussion so far, there is one important item that has not been mentioned: how much did we borrow (how much did the bond-holder lend) with the bond? One possible answer is £100. This is because we will be paying back this amount to the lender – the face value – when the bond matures. However, this is only one possibility. For instance, we may borrow £80 and still pay £100 in face value and the four coupon payments. In this case, it is clear that the bond buyer is going to make a higher return because, in addition to making money on the coupons to be received, this lender will get the difference between the amount of money lent to us (£80) and what we promise to pay when the bond expires (£100).

Alternatively, we could agree with the bond buyer to lend us £120 and subsequently pay the four coupons and the face value of £100. In this event, the lender would get a lower return. But why would the lender agree to settle for less? A possible answer is that the lender is going to get a good return from the coupons. The key point here is that the amount we borrow does not have to be the same as the face value.

Answering the question of how much we are borrowing effectively means calculating how much a potential bond buyer would be willing to lend us. Let's first try to figure out how much this bond is worth. Taking into account the concept of the time value of money covered in Chapter 2, the money that the lender can expect to receive from the bond is shown in Figure 5.3.

	Now		2018		2019		2020		2021	
Year	0		1		2		3		4	
Coupon		£	10	£	10	£	10	£	10	
Face value										100
Total		£	10	£	10	£	10	£	110	

Figure 5.3 Calculation of bond price

Discounting the coupons and face value, the calculation is shown in Equation 5.1.

How much the bond is worth

$$= \frac{£10}{(1+r)} + \frac{£10}{(1+r)^2} + \frac{£10}{(1+r)^3} + \frac{£10+£100}{(1+r)^4} \tag{5.1}$$

What should be the discount rate that we use? It should definitely not be the coupon rate, as this rate is used only to calculate the size of the coupons. The correct discount rate to use in bond price calculation is called *yield to maturity* (YTM), or simply yield. So, if the YTM is, say, 12 per cent, the answer to the equation would be £93.93, as shown in Equation 5.2.

$$\frac{£10}{(1+12\%)} + \frac{£10}{(1+12\%)^2} + \frac{£10}{(1+12\%)^3}$$
$$+ \frac{£10+£100}{(1+12\%)^4} = £93.93 \tag{5.2}$$

There are different ways to interpret this but, ultimately, they all point to the same idea. In finance jargon, the answer £93.93 is called the *bond price* – that is, how much this bond is worth should one want to buy or sell it. For example, if we are selling this bond, we are effectively handing over the bond and receiving £93.93 from the bond buyer. In other words, we are borrowing this amount and, with the bond, we promise to pay £10 of coupons each year for the next 4 years and £100 when the bond matures.

So, in this situation, how big is the return the buyer is getting? The answer is 12 per cent. In other words, YTM effectively shows the return that bond investors get. But what happens if the lender thinks we are a risky borrower and is only willing to lend us money if she can get a 20 per cent return? In this case, as shown in Equation 5.3, we can only borrow £74.11. This means that we have to sell the bond at the price of £74.11, so as to offer a 20 per cent return and make the bond sufficiently attractive to the buyer.

$$\frac{£10}{(1+20\%)} + \frac{£10}{(1+20\%)^2} + \frac{£10}{(1+20\%)^3}$$
$$+ \frac{£10+£100}{(1+20\%)^4} = £74.11 \tag{5.3}$$

All of these examples highlight at least three important points about bonds.

First, the price of the bond (how much it is worth) today is the total of the discounted value of the future coupons and face value. The generic formula for bond calculation is shown in Equation 5.4, where n denotes the number of periods.

$$Bond\ price = \frac{Coupon}{(1+YTM)} + \frac{Coupon}{(1+YTM)^2} + \frac{Coupon}{(1+YTM)^3}$$
$$+ \cdots \frac{Coupon + Face\ value}{(1+YTM)^n} \tag{5.4}$$

As a side point, bond coupons are usually not paid on an annual basis, but more commonly every 6 months. The calculation of the price of a bond with semi-annual coupons has to take into account the different time periods, the coupon size and the YTM. Equation 5.5 shows the generic formula for such a calculation, where n denotes the number of 6-month periods.

$$Bond\ price = \frac{Coupon \div 2}{(1+YTM \div 2)} + \frac{Coupon \div 2}{(1+YTM \div 2)^2}$$
$$+ \cdots \frac{Coupon \div 2 + Face\ value}{(1+YTM \div 2)^n} \tag{5.5}$$

Second, YTM is the return that investors require to be willing to buy the bond (i.e. lend money). Like an interest rate on a bank loan, YTM – from the perspective of the sellers (like us) – represents the cost of using bonds.

Conversely, from the viewpoint of investors, YTM is the return needed by these bondholders. This "two sides of the same coin" for bonds is summarised in Table 5.3.

Third, unlike bank loans, there is not just one way, but two ways, for investors to obtain their return. These are:

1   Coupons and
2   The difference between the bond price and face value (It is probably easier to think about this as the difference between what you lend out and what you get paid back. If you get paid back more than what you lent out, then you must be making a gain.)

Table 5.3 Two sides of the same coin (bank loans and bonds)

	From the company's viewpoint . . .	From the investors' viewpoint . . .
Bank loan: The interest rate is the . . .	Cost of using the bank loan	Return needed by the bank
Bond: The YTM is the . . .	Cost of using the bond	Return needed by the bondholder/investor

This point is particularly important due to a special characteristic of bonds: they can be bought/sold or traded. Let's assume that Bob has just bought the bond issued by us. Since he knows us well, he is willing to accept a return of 12 per cent. In this case, he pays £93.93 for the bond. However, shortly after this transaction, he suddenly needs money and cannot wait 4 years before getting his money back. So, he tries to sell the bond to Charlie. But Charlie wants a higher return, possibly because she does not know us very well and, thus, considers that buying the bond that we issued is risky. At what price should Bob sell the bond, given what the bond promises to pay in the next 4 years? Let's say Bob knows that Charlie wants a return of 20 per cent.

This means that he will find a way to give Charlie the extra return that she requires. Yet, Bob cannot alter the coupon rate. This is because it was predetermined when we issued the bond. Therefore, the only way that he can provide Charlie with the return she needs is by lowering the price of the bond when selling it to her. Hence, Bob will have to sell the bond for £74.11 to offer her a high enough return to take it off his hands.

We can assume that, if Bob is rational, he will not sell the bond to Charlie at *less* than £74.11 – why offer a higher return (and lose more money) than necessary? Nor will Bob be able to sell the bond to Charlie at *more* than £74.11, as she would not get the return she needs and, hence, will decide against buying the bond.

Let's use another example to illustrate this concept further. Many governments in the world borrow money by issuing bonds. When individuals (usually their citizens) or companies buy these bonds, they are effectively lending money to the issuing governments. However, most of these government bonds do not pay any coupons.

Therefore, these bonds are a form of *zero-coupon bonds*. So, how are the buyers getting their return? The answer should be clear by now: they obtain their rewards from receiving more than they lent out. For instance, if a government sells a bond at £90 and promises to pay back £100 a year from now, the return that the bond investors would get is 11.11 per cent, as stated in Equation 5.6.

$$\frac{£100}{(1+YTM)} = £90 \qquad (5.6)$$
$$YTM = 11.11\%$$

THE (INVERSE) RELATIONSHIP BETWEEN BOND PRICE AND YTM

If the government bond is not sold at £90 but rather at £83, what happens to the return to the bond investors? The answer: the return would be around 12 per cent. When the bond price comes down, YTM goes up. The opposite is also true. When the bond price increases, YTM decreases. In other words, there is an inverse relationship between bond price and YTM. It should be clear by now that the only way to offer a higher (lower) return to investors is to decrease (increase) the price to create a bigger (smaller) difference between the price and the face value.

FACTORS DETERMINING THE RETURN THAT THE LENDERS REQUIRE

At this stage, a logical question could be: "What determines YTM (i.e. the return the investors need)?" There are numerous factors that influence the yield that bondholders get. The most important ones are available alternatives, the borrower's credentials and market views.

Available alternatives

A bond investor, Charlie, will buy a bond (lend money) when the bond provides the return that she requires. Rationally, she will compare the bond return to the return that other borrowers in the market will offer her. Let's say she has a choice between keeping the money in the bank and collecting 3 per cent interest. (Let's not forget that, in this case, the investor is merely lending the money to the bank in exchange for interest.) Let's assume further that she is willing to buy a bond if it can give her a 10 per cent return. In this case, Charlie is effectively asking for an additional 7 per cent to compensate for the extra risk-taking when buying this bond. To her, anything less would not be enough to justify the risk of investing in this bond.

So, if the interest rate that the bank offers went up from 3 to 4 per cent, it would deem a 6 per cent difference between the two investment choices insufficient to justify the amount of risk taken. In this case, she would require an 11 per cent yield on the bond instead of only 10 per cent.

But what can be driving the bank interest rate up in the first place? One answer is that bank interest rates usually go up and down with the base rates – the interest rates set by the Bank of England. Therefore, when the Bank of England raises the base rate, the return that many investment alternatives offer goes up (including that of bank accounts and bonds).

Reversing the operation, if the Bank of England lowers the base rate, the return that many investment possibilities provide (including what a bank account can offer) decreases. As the alternative lending opportunities become less attractive, the bond becomes a good deal and many other investors become attracted by this relatively higher yield. As a result of an increased number of buyers, the price of the bond goes up, eventually bringing down the rate of return.

Borrower's credentials

The higher the risk that a borrower presents, the higher the return a lender will demand. Assume there are two companies, A and B. Company A has a high probability of going bankrupt, whereas company B is unlikely to go out of business. In this case, the default risk (the risk that the company will be unable to pay the interest/ coupons and the lent amount) is much higher for company A than B. Consequently, lenders will demand a much higher return to lend money to company A than to B. This is also where the credit rating agencies play a role. These agencies – including Standard & Poor's, Moody's and Fitch – assess the quality of the bonds that companies want to issue, thereby providing potential investors with objective expert opinions on the likelihood that the bond issuing companies will be able to honour their promises. The safer the bond, the fewer investors are able to ask for a higher return. Hence, bond issuers such as company B can have a lower cost of borrowing.

Market views

When buying bonds, investors are concerned with more than just whether the bond issuers would pay the coupons and face value. They also care about how easy (or difficult) it is to sell the bond in case they have to. Whether there is an active market for the bonds to be traded thus influences the amount of risk that the investors bear. So, if an investor wants to offload a bond during the holding period, and there are only a few takers because, say, the borrower or the bond is relatively unknown, she will only be able to sell it at a low price, so as to appeal to buyers. In this case, this investor would demand a higher return, and hence a higher YTM, from the bond issuers at the time of purchase to compensate for the "lack of market".

IMPLICATIONS OF DEBT ON CAPITAL STRUCTURE

Now that we have covered both bank loans and bonds, let's see how debt plays a crucial role in the capital structure of any company through leverage and tax benefits.

Leverage

A concept that many people have heard of but know little about is leverage. Leverage is about using debt to achieve a certain outcome. Let's consider the following two scenarios, as illustrated in Figure 5.4, to understand it better.

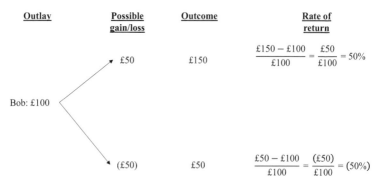

Figure 5.4 Scenario 1 – Rates of return without leverage

Scenario 1: A project requires an upfront investment of £100 and has a 50/50 probability of reaching a "good" or "bad" outcome a year later. With the good outcome, the project will reward £50 on top of the £100 outlay. In contrast, with the bad outcome, the project will lead to a loss of £50. Bob is to finance the investment with £100 of his own money. What would be the rate of return for Bob in each case?

In the first case, Bob gets £150 (i.e. £50 of gain in addition to the £100 initial investment) at the end of the project. Deducting the outlay of £100, Bob's rate of return is 50 per cent. In the second case, the project ends with only £50, representing a loss of £50. Dividing it by £100, Bob experiences a rate of loss of 50 per cent (or a rate of return of negative 50 per cent).

Scenario 2: The project and its possible outcomes are *exactly* the same as in the previous scenario. The sole difference is in how Bob finances the initial £100 needed. In this case, Charlie is extending him a loan of £80 for 1 year at an interest rate of 20 per cent. Bob therefore only needs to spend £20 of his own money and pays £16 (£80 × 20%) in interest after 1 year.

Figure 5.5 shows the calculations of the two possibilities.

In the "gain" outcome, Bob gets £150 at the end of the project. Unlike in scenario 1, more than one deduction needs to be made, including £16 of interest and the £80 repayment to Charlie, as well as Bob's £20 outlay. This all leads to a final amount of £34. But here is the trickier part: what should this £34 of return be divided by? It is not £100. Why? Because, unlike in scenario 1 (where the £100

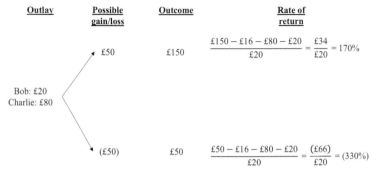

Figure 5.5 Scenario 2 – Rates of return with debt leverage

outlay is fully funded by Bob), the financing arrangement is made up of both Bob's own money and Charlie's loan. To answer the question, let's ask who is entitled to the £34. Rightfully, it belongs to Bob only. This is because Charlie has already got her investment (the loan of £80) as well as her return (the £16 interest) when going through the deductions. So, to determine the rate of return, the £34 is divided by Bob's contribution to the project outlay, which is £20. The rate of return is therefore 170 per cent! Running through the same logic, in the "loss" outcome, Bob's rate of return would be a whopping *negative* 330 per cent!

How can the huge difference in the rates of return between the two scenarios, even though the project in both cases has exactly the same characteristics, be explained? A couple of observations can be made:

1   Debt amplifies both gains and losses. In comparison to Bob, Charlie makes a 20 per cent return in the second scenario from the interest, *regardless* of the eventual outcome that Bob faces. Figure 5.6 compares the returns that both Bob and Charlie can obtain.

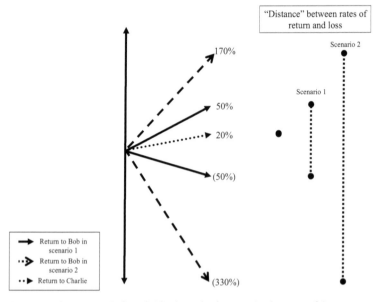

Figure 5.6 Returns to Bob and Charlie in both scenarios (not to scale)

2   From the previous point, regardless of the final project outcome, Charlie is set to make a gain from receiving interest. In essence, she has not been exposed to any of the risks of Bob's investment.[2] Bob, therefore, is the sole bearer of the risk of the investment in the project. Recall that high risk should be accompanied by a higher return; the 170 per cent return when using debt (as opposed to 50 per cent without) represents such compensation. Nonetheless, Bob can also lose a great deal more if the investment does not go well. Therefore, the distance between the possible rates of return and loss in both scenarios (as shown by the vertical lines on the right-hand side of Figure 5.6) represents the risk. This points to an important aspect of corporate finance: risk is neither good nor bad. It merely describes volatility, which basically means a higher chance of making or losing more than expected (more on this concept in the next chapter). The vertical line for scenario 2 is longer than that for scenario 1, denoting that there is a possibility of making a substantial gain, but equally, it is possible to lose a lot. Compare this to the vertical line of scenario 1, which has lower risk (losing no more than 50 per cent) but also lower possible gain (making no more than 50 per cent). As a final note, since Charlie is not exposed to any risk in the investment of this project and hence bears none of its volatility, the representation of her investment does not have a line at all – only a dot.

This example demonstrates, in effect, the essence of financial engineering. Bob's boosted gain does not come from improving the outcomes of a project. The single source of increased return is the way the project is financed. In the first scenario, Bob finances the investment purely with equity – his own money. In the second case, he finances it partially with debt and partially with equity. Bob has simply used debt to boost the return he can gain from equity. Indeed, the higher the debt component of the financing, the higher the risk and therefore the higher the potential return.

It is now possible to answer the question: what is leverage? In this example, through the use of debt, Bob manages to boost his return on the money that he has invested in the project. Effectively, he has used debt to enhance his return as the owner of the investment. Leverage is therefore about boosting the return on equity through the use of debt.

Company A (Without debt)			Company B (With debt)		
Interest rate:		0%	Interest rate:		20%
Rate for all taxes:		40%	Rate for all taxes:		40%
EBIT	£	100	EBIT	£	100
Interest		-	Interest		20
EBT		100	EBT		80
Taxes		40	Taxes		32
Net income	£	60	Net income	£	48

Figure 5.7 Tax benefits

Tax benefits

There is another benefit to using debt as a means of financing. Businesses pay less tax when borrowing. Recall that, following the current accounting conventions, companies pay interest *before* paying taxes. Consider the two income statements in Figure 5.7.

The only difference between the two cases is that company B has used debt and therefore must pay interest. The result is that, even though both companies make the same amount of money operationally, company B pays £8 less in taxes. Viewed differently, the current accounting standard is effectively incentivising companies to take on debt.

What about the net income to the shareholders? Are company B's shareholders losing out, as it is clear that they are making *less* than those in company A with the use of debt? No, because they are benefiting from the leverage effect. Given the shareholders in company B will need to put *less* capital forward, they will see their rate of return going up, even though they are getting less in net income in absolute terms. This is the same as Bob making only £34 in scenario 2 instead of £50, as the above illustration of leverage shows. He is still making more as a return in this case because he only needs to put in £20 as opposed to £100.

SUMMARY

This chapter has described and explored the characteristics of loans and bonds. In particular, it has discussed the various components of bonds and how they affect bond value. The best way to understand how bonds work is to understand that, unlike bank loans (through which there is only one way to provide a return, in the form of interest), bonds offer two possibilities through which to do so – coupons and the difference between the borrowed amount (bond price) and the repayment amount (face value). These two sources of gains boil down to the rate of return, called *yield*. In other words, the return on a bond or the cost of using it is often a matter of how the bonds are structured around these gains.

This chapter has also examined the implications of debt on a company's capital structure through looking at leverage and tax benefits. But, as the concept of leverage should have made it clear, debt is closely related to shareholders' equity. So, what exactly is equity? This is the topic we turn to in the next chapter.

NOTES

1 Naturally, this process is now being done by technology.
2 So, why is Charlie getting a 20 per cent return? Even though it is not related to Bob's investment, such a return represents compensation for the risk of lending to Bob but not for the potential outcomes of the project.

EQUITY

CHAPTER OVERVIEW

Lenders are only one of the two major investors in a business. Owners fund businesses too, as they get a part of the business – or shares – in exchange for the capital provided. However, unlike lenders, who usually receive fixed rewards periodically, shareholders receive the profit generated by the business when the business performs well. When the company is struggling and losing money, the shareholders have to bear any losses incurred. This shows that, like Bob in the discussion of leverage in the previous chapter, shareholders are exposed to higher risk, which entitles them to a potentially higher return. This chapter looks more closely at equity and, specifically, at determining the cost of equity. After that, it discusses how to combine the cost of using different financing options in order to establish the cost of capital of a business.

CHARACTERISTICS OF SHAREHOLDERS' EQUITY

Let's explore the characteristics of shareholders' equity in greater depth (see Figure 6.1).

In "bad" times, the company makes little money (£10) from its operations but a lot more in "good" times (£1,000). The company

	"Bad"	"Normal"	"Good"
EBIT	£10	£100	£1,000
Interest	10	10	10
Earnings before taxes	0	90	990
Taxes (at 50%)	0	45	495
Net income	0	£45	495

Figure 6.1 Shareholders' gains in different performance situations

has to pay £10 of interest, regardless of the state of the business. Since debtholders are not profit-sharing with the shareholders, their gain is restricted to the £10 interest paid by the company. To see how this affects the shareholders, it is important to recall that, as noted in Chapter 1, debtholders are the first to be paid and shareholders the last. This arrangement makes a difference.

Consider the "bad" situation. In this case, the company has only managed to make £10 from its operational activities and must pay it all out as interest. This leaves the shareholders with nothing. In contrast, in the "good" state, when the business does well and makes £1,000 in EBIT, the shareholders are entitled to all of the remaining amount of £495 after interest and taxes have been paid.

This demonstration shows that, whereas debtholders are getting a stable income, the gains to the shareholders are subject to income fluctuation (or volatility) and therefore risk. In our example, they can gain as little as nothing or as much as £495. Consequently, they are rewarded with a potentially higher return than that of debtholders. Indeed, if the company is really performing poorly, the shareholders are the investors who have to absorb the losses. Shareholders' equity is considered the most "junior" type of financing: being junior, shareholders are paid last. Being junior also means that, if the company goes bankrupt, the proceeds from the sale of the company's assets will go first to paying back the debtholders *in full*. Only if there is anything left will it then go towards compensating the shareholders.

Two important insights emerge here. First, in just the same way as the cost of debt and the return that the lenders require are two sides of the same coin, the cost of equity and the return needed by the shareholders represent different perspectives on the same matter, as shown in Table 6.1.

Second, given that the shareholders will always ask for a higher return as a result of the higher risk they face, the cost of using equity will always be higher than the cost of debt, i.e.:

Cost of equity > Cost of debt

Or simply:

$$r_E > r_D$$

Let's now look at how to calculate the cost of equity.

Table 6.1 Two sides of the same coin (bank loans, bonds and equity)

	From the company's viewpoint . . .	*From the investors' viewpoint . . .*
Bank loan: The interest rate is the . . .	Cost of using the bank loan	Return needed by the bank
Bond: The YTM is the . . .	Cost of using the bond	Return needed by the bondholder/investor
Equity: The dividend growth model or the CAPM (both described below) leads to the . . .	Cost of equity	Return needed by the shareholders

DETERMINING THE COST OF EQUITY

The cost of equity can be established by figuring out the return that the shareholders would want. There are generally two possible methods.

Method 1: dividend growth model

The first approach is the dividend growth model (also called the *Gordon-Shapiro model*). The best starting point for understanding this model is to look at how shareholders can make money from investing in a company. Typically, they do so from 1) receiving dividends from the company and 2) selling their shares at a price higher than the price they paid for them in the first place (i.e. capital gains). In this case, arguably, the price of a share today must be attributable to the future dividends and share price. This idea is captured in Equation 6.1.

$$P_0 = \frac{(D_1 + P_1)}{(1+r)} \tag{6.1}$$

The price of a share today (P_0) is composed of the dividend to be paid next year (D_1) plus the expected price of the share next year (P_1). Since they are both due next year, they will have to be discounted in order to reach today's price.

Whereas next year's dividend can be estimated with some confidence because it can be based on the amount of dividend paid this year, determining the share price next year is more difficult. One way to get around this is to argue that next year's share price will be shaped by the dividend paid and share price in year 2, which can be represented by Equation 6.2.

$$P_1 = \frac{(D_2 + P_2)}{(1+r)} \tag{6.2}$$

In this equation, the dividend and share price in year 2 are only discounted for 1 year because they are used for the calculation of the year 1 share price. But how can we get an estimate of P_2? Well, similarly to year 2, it is equal to the discounted value of the year 3 dividend and share price. In turn, P_3 depends on the dividend and share price of year 4 and so on.

If we continue with this logic and integrate Equations 6.1 and 6.2, it becomes clear that the price of a share today is the discounted value of *all* the dividends in the future. Unless there is a good reason, potential investors of equity would normally assume that the company will exist forever and therefore distribute dividends forever. This is shown in Equation 6.3.

$$P_0 = \frac{D_1}{(1+r)} + \frac{D_2}{(1+r)^2} + \frac{D_3}{(1+r)^3} + \frac{D_4}{(1+r)^4} + \cdots \infty \tag{6.3}$$

But how do we predict the size of the dividends in the future years? Understandably, it is very difficult (if not impossible) to determine the dividend size, particularly for those that are far into the future. In this case, various assumptions have to be made.

Assumption no. 1

One possibility is to assume that the company will pay *exactly* the same amount of dividend every year infinitely (i.e. $D_1 = D_2 = D_3 = D_4$ and so on), which means that all future gains will remain the same forever. Applying the perpetuity formula discussed in the appendix of Chapter 2, the share price today in this case can be calculated as shown in Equation 6.4.

$$P_0 = \frac{D_1}{r} \qquad (6.4)$$

Assumption no. 2

While our example essentially assumes that the company does not grow its activities at all (and therefore generates the same amount of profit and dividends every year), in reality many companies do grow. Therefore, another approach to estimating the share price today is to assume a certain rate of stable growth. The calculation of today's share price thus becomes Equation 6.5.

$$P_0 = \frac{D_1}{r - g} \qquad (6.5)$$

It is hereby assumed that dividends will forever increase at a fixed rate of g every year, starting from year 1 to year 2 (e.g. $D_2 = D_1 \times (1 + g)$ and $D_3 = D_2 \times (1 + g)$ etc.).

Equation 6.5 is essentially the dividend growth model. This model, however, comes with two main caveats. First, it assumes that the company currently pays dividends. In reality, many businesses – including those that grow – do not. Why? Imagine that Bob is the CEO of a fast-growing tech company. Imagine further that he can choose to pay shareholders in dividends (in cash) or to put this cash back into the company for further investment. If Bob anticipates that the business has plenty of value-creating opportunities ahead, which would generate more money for the shareholders in the form of an increased share price in the future than the dividends paid out today, he can make a strong case to these investors to give up all the dividends and let him put the money back into growing the business. Put differently, the shareholders can be better off *not* receiving dividends today so as to gain more in the future in the form of an increased share price.

The reverse is also true. Businesses that face limited (but not zero) growth prospects, such as those in mature industries, are much less able to convince their shareholders that they should retain the dividends for reinvestment because there are few value-creating opportunities that could lift the share price significantly. In this respect, the dividend growth model is perhaps more applicable to established companies and far less suitable for start-ups and growing businesses.

The second caveat is that it is very difficult, if not impossible, to establish what a realistic growth rate should be, especially when the growth rate in this model represents the average rate at which the company will grow *forever*.

Given these two limitations, the dividend growth model may seem of little practical use. But it has at least one important merit: it can help estimate the rate of return that shareholders are expecting and, therefore, the cost of equity. To see how these two concepts are related, let's rearrange the dividend growth model as shown in Equation 6.6.

$$P_0 = \frac{D_1}{r - g}$$
$$P_0 \times (r - g) = D_1$$
$$r - g = \frac{D_1}{P_0} \tag{6.6}$$
$$r = \frac{D_1}{P_0} + g$$

The r in this equation must be the rate of return that the shareholders get and, hence, the cost of equity. Why? Because they are the only investors who are entitled to receive dividends. Hence, if we replace r with r_E, the cost of equity equals next year's dividends divided by the share price today plus the average perpetual growth rate, as shown in Equation 6.7.

$$r_E = \frac{D_1}{P_0} + g \tag{6.7}$$

In conclusion, the dividend growth model can help companies determine the cost of equity, but the limited practicalities of the model do not make it a popular tool among companies. Managers often turn to another method called the *capital asset pricing model* (or CAPM).

Capital asset pricing model (CAPM)

Unlike the previous model, CAPM estimates the return required by shareholders from an "external" perspective. The calculation is shown in Equation 6.8.

$$r_E = r_f + \beta(r_m - r_f) \tag{6.8}$$

In this formula, r_f refers to the risk-free rate, whereas r_m represents the market return. β (called *beta*) measures how risky a company's share is compared to the overall market risk. In order to understand what CAPM describes, we first need to look at four concepts:

1   Risk and return
2   Diversification through portfolio
3   Non-systematic risk versus systematic risk
4   Beta

We will then see how, together, they make up CAPM.

1) Risk and return

Let's get one concept right at the outset. Risk and return, in theory, go hand in hand. This means that the higher the risk an investor faces, the higher the potential return (or loss) this investor is expecting. So, if you were lending money to Greece in 2016 (by buying its government bonds), you would have asked for a higher return than if you were lending to Germany. That is simply because there is a higher chance that Greece, compared to Germany, would not be able to pay you back.

The same idea applies to buying the shares of small businesses versus those of large corporations. Imagine that an investor can invest either in a start-up with huge potential growth or in a blue chip corporation – a big company with a global reputation for quality, reliability and the ability to operate profitably in good times and bad.

One major difference between these two options is the risk: the start-up may be operating in an unchartered, yet potentially profitable, market in which there is very little competition at the moment. By doing something novel, it may make a lot of money. But, equally, given that it is operating on untested grounds, there is a chance that it can fail and the shareholders might lose their investment.

By contrast, investing in a large corporation that has been earning a stable income in a more established market makes it less likely for the investor to lose money, but it is unlikely that the returns it offers can be on par with those of a successful start-up in its early stages. In other words, high-potential early-stage businesses have a higher probability of both losing *and* making a lot of money for their shareholders. In comparison, investments in large, established companies have a far smaller range of losses and gains.

This illustrates a very important point: the concept of risk is often misunderstood. It often carries a negative connotation. Yet, inherently, risk is neither bad nor good. Take, for instance, a share that is traded on the stock market. Historically, it has provided, on average, a 12 per cent return a year. Since this return is an average, in some years the share only offers, say, a 6 per cent return, whereas in others it offers 18 per cent. Yet, when people talk about risk, they usually think only of the *downsides* of getting a 6 per cent return. The potential *upside* of an 18 per cent gain is never seen as a risk. What the term "risk" actually describes is the full range of possibilities of experiencing both the downside losses *and* the upside gains. Put another way, in our example, risk is related to both "sides" of the average 12 per cent gain.

Following the above logic, it is possible to come to the following conclusion: to find out how risky an investment is, we can look at the probability of *not* getting the return expected. The higher this probability, the higher the risk!

2) Diversification through portfolio

An important concept in finance is diversification. To understand this, let's assume company ABC has historically provided its shareholders with a return of 10 per cent. So, if Charlie invests her money and buys a share of ABC, she can expect to get a return of 10 per cent. Now, let's consider another company called DEF, which has been offering a 15 per cent return to its shareholders in the past (the higher return offered suggests it would be a riskier investment than ABC). What happens if Charlie also invests in DEF, creating a two-asset *portfolio*?

It depends on how much Charlie is investing in each of the companies. For example, if, out of £10,000 available for investment, she decides to put £6,000 in ABC and the remainder in DEF, the return she can expect from her portfolio would be 12 per cent, as shown in Equation 6.9.

$$\begin{aligned} &\textit{Expected return on Charlie's portfolio} \\ &\quad = 60\% \times 10\% + 40\% \times 15\% = 12\% \end{aligned} \tag{6.9}$$

As can be imagined, the more of the £10,000 Charlie allocates to investing in DEF, the higher the return from the portfolio she can potentially get. In fact, if Charlie allocates 100 per cent of her £10,000 to DEF, she can expect to make the highest return (15 per cent) out of her investment. So, why would she not do this and forget about ABC altogether? The answer lies in the risk of her portfolio.

According to financial theory, the risk of a portfolio depends on several elements:

- The proportion of money invested in each company. In this example, the more Charlie invests in the riskier DEF, the higher the overall risk of her portfolio.
- The risk of the individual company's shares. In this case, how risky ABC and DEF are, respectively.
- The correlation between ABC and DEF.

The last point is important. Without having to delve deep into statistics, correlation describes how the returns of ABC and of DEF are related. This is calculated by observing how, historically, the shares of the two companies have been moving in the same direction together. Following statistics, the correlation between the return on two companies will always have a value between −1 and +1.

As shown in Figure 6.2, on one end of the spectrum it is possible that, when ABC is generating a positive return, DEF's return will *always* be negative. In this case, the correlation is said to be −1. At the opposite end of the spectrum, when the return on ABC is positive, that on DEF will *always* be positive (a correlation of +1). Right in the middle of the spectrum lays the situation where the return on ABC is positive. It is impossible to conclude whether the return on DEF

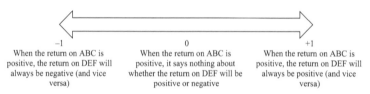

Figure 6.2 Possibilities for the relationship between ABC and DEF

will be positive or negative (the correlation is 0). There is simply no correlation between them.

An important outcome with this observation is that, according to financial theory, with a portfolio containing two shares that have a negative correlation, investors can eliminate – or, in corporate finance parlance, diversify away – some of the risk. Put differently, if ABC and DEF are negatively correlated, by holding a portfolio with these two shares, Charlie can get rid of some of the risk, while making a decent return.

Let's take this a step further. If risk *diversification* can be achieved with two shares, what happens if Charlie adds a third one? Theory has shown that she can see the risk of her portfolio further reduced. In fact, if she were to include a fourth one, the risk of her portfolio would diminish even more! So, if Charlie kept on adding shares into her portfolio to achieve ever-more diversification, would she ultimately be able to completely eliminate all the risk on her portfolio? The answer is, of course, no. Otherwise, all investors in history would have already used this approach. Why is it impossible to completely diversify all the risk away? The reason is that there are generally two types of risk: non-systematic and systematic.

3) Non-systematic versus systematic risk

Non-systematic risk is risk associated with individual companies, for instance, with specific projects and strategies. *Systematic risk* is risk that is not caused by the actions of individual companies. It is the risk that results from the national or global economic and business environment.

As illustrated in Figure 6.3, holding a portfolio can only reduce non-systematic risk. Once a portfolio has 25 to 30 shares there will be no additional effect from diversification, as most of the non-systematic risk will have been eliminated. On the other hand, diversification has no effect on systematic risk. If the world economy were going through a recession, most (if not all) shares would be affected by the economic downturn. Therefore, holding shares in many individual companies in a portfolio would not enable any investor to be rid of the risk related to the wider environment.

Two implications can be drawn from the discussion here. First, investors are able to use portfolios to diversify away, in theory at least,

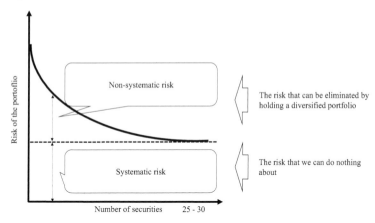

Figure 6.3 Non-systematic risk versus systematic risk

all the non-systematic risk. Second, by holding a portfolio, the only risk that investors face but cannot do anything about is the systematic risk. This means that it is crucial for us to be able to measure this risk.

4) Beta

Enter beta. Beta measures the systematic risk of a company's share in comparison to that of the whole market. It therefore gives a sense of a share's risk vis-à-vis the greater market. A company with a beta of 1 means that it is just as volatile as the market. If a company has a beta greater than 1, it shows that the company's share is more volatile than the market. The opposite is true if beta is smaller than 1. To illustrate this, consider a mining company that has a beta of 2. A 2 means its share is twice as volatile as the market. What does this mean? This means that, if the market is seeing a 1 per cent gain, shareholders of this mining company should expect a return of 2 per cent.

To determine the "market" return, people tend to use a stock market index such as the FTSE 100 (which is made up of the 100 largest companies traded on the London Stock Exchange) as a proxy for the wider market. So, going back to the example, if the return on the FTSE 100 is −2 per cent, then we can anticipate a return of −4 per cent for our mining company. The reason why both the gains and losses are amplified is that, when the economy is doing well, mining companies tend to do better given the increased demand for minerals and raw materials. In contrast, if the economy is in a recession, a mining company's performance is likely to be hit because there will be much less demand for its products.

Now, consider the beta of an energy provider. It is more likely to be around 1, meaning the company has the same systematic risk as the market as a whole. This is because energy is essential whether the economy is in a state of boom or bust. Hence, if the return on the FTSE 100 goes up by 1 per cent, the return on this energy provider will go up by roughly the same (i.e. by approximately 1 per cent). Neither gains nor losses are amplified.

One question many newcomers to corporate finance ask is how to obtain beta. The answer is rather simple: it is published on financial information websites, including Google Finance and Bloomberg.com. It must be noted, however, that the beta published can actually vary from one source to another. This is because the betas on different sites are estimated in different ways. Regardless, they should not be distinctively different from each other and, thus, give a sense of a company's systematic risk.

Revisiting CAPM

Having gone through the key concepts underpinning CAPM, we can bring them together to see how it is calculated and how it helps us to figure out the cost of equity. As a reminder, the CAPM formula is repeated in Equation 6.10.

$$r_E = r_f + \beta \ (r_m - r_f) \tag{6.10}$$

CAPM starts with r_f (or risk-free investments). These are investments that have got no risk (i.e. a guaranteed income with zero probability of making anything more or less). What kind of investments are free of risk? Bonds issued by governments. Granted, not all government bonds have no risk. However, some are considered virtually risk-free – such as those in the US and Germany – because, if governments cannot service the interest or pay back the borrowed amount, they can always resort to printing more money to do so. For sure, it can be argued that this introduces inflation. However, ultimately, the government has promised the lenders that they will get their money back. But how much the money is worth is a different story altogether. Since these bonds carry no risk in this sense, their return tends to be lower than those of all other risky financial instruments.

CAPM starts with risk-free investments for a very logical reason: an investor will only be interested in making a risky investment – for instance, buying a share – if she is getting at least what risk-free government bonds can offer. The second part of the formula, then, relates to what return she can get *in addition* to that from risk-free government bonds.

Let's break it down. r_m (market return) represents the return that an investor can get from investing in the market (such as the FTSE 100, as discussed above). So, the $r_m - r_f$ is called the *market risk premium* and represents the extra reward for taking the risk to invest in the market. Lastly, this additional gain depends on the systematic risk and is therefore multiplied by beta. Said differently, a company with a higher systematic risk should provide its investors with a higher return.

So all in all, CAPM shows how much return an investor expects from a company's share. It depends on the return on risk-free investment, the return on the market (i.e. FTSE 100) and the company's systematic risk relative to the market's.

Two different methods to estimate the cost of equity – the dividend growth model and CAPM – are presented here. CAPM is the more popular approach, not least because the former model has limitations. Furthermore, the information needed (i.e. on the returns of risk-free government bonds and the FTSE 100, as well as companies' beta) to calculate CAPM is readily accessible by the public. Consequently, CAPM is often better accepted as the tool to estimate cost of equity.

CAPM for small, private businesses

Assume for the moment that you want to find the cost of equity of a publicly traded restaurant chain using CAPM. Since it is a public company, it is possible to use the beta information that is widely published. But what do you do if you want to figure out the cost of equity for a private restaurant that is not publicly traded? There is no publicly available data and, therefore, the beta information is absent in this case.

To circumvent this, one common practice is to use the beta of the publicly traded company that is closest in nature to the private business in question. Using CAPM, the resulting cost of equity is then adjusted. For instance, for small or private businesses, a popular approach is to add an extra 3 to 5 per cent to CAPM based on the assumption that these businesses are more risky than their larger counterparts and, hence, have a higher cost of equity.

WEIGHTED AVERAGE COST OF CAPITAL

Now it is possible to establish the cost of capital of a company that uses both debt *and* equity. The method often used to do so is called *weighted average cost of capital* (or simply WACC), as shown in Equation 6.11, where w_E refers to the weight of equity, w_D the weight of debt and t the tax rate.

$$WACC = w_E r_E + w_D r_D (1 - t) \tag{6.11}$$

The sum of w_D and w_E must be 100 per cent. Once again, r_E and r_D are the cost of equity and the cost of debt, respectively.

The weight of equity (w_E) and the weight of debt (w_D) depend on the composition of a company's capital. For instance, if a company has a total of £1 million injected by investors, with 30 per cent being made up of debt and the rest coming from equity, w_D and w_E will be 30 per cent and 70 per cent, respectively. r_D and r_E can be calculated using the methods presented in this chapter and the previous one. Lastly, the reason why there is a $(1 - t)$ applied on the debt part of the WACC equation is that, as pointed out in the previous chapter, debt benefits from tax advantages because interest is paid out before corporate tax is paid. Equity does not have such a privilege.

Two important points need to be highlighted. First, if a company uses different types of financial instruments to form its capital, its WACC has to take all of them into account. For example, if a company is financed by a bank loan, bonds and equity, its WACC has to consider this makeup accordingly, as demonstrated in Equation 6.12, where BA represents bank loans and BO bonds.

$$WACC = w_E r_E + w_{BA} r_{BA} (1 - t) + w_{BO} r_{BO} (1 - t) \tag{6.12}$$

Naturally, the sum of the three weights has to be 100 per cent. Also, $(1 - t)$ is applied to both bank loans and bonds because they are both debt instruments.

Second, as discussed at the beginning of this chapter, debt as a means of financing is always cheaper than equity. So, as r_D is always smaller than r_E, a company that uses a great deal of debt can substantially lower its WACC. On top of this, the tax advantages accorded to debt decrease the WACC even further. An important implication is that the more debt there is, the lower the cost of capital. In turn, the lower the cost of capital, the higher the NPV will be! This is one reason why many businesses find debt financing so attractive.

BRINGING NPV, FCF AND WACC TOGETHER

As discussed in Chapter 2, a positive net present value (NPV), resulting from discounting future free cash flows, indicates to a business that an investment is worth undertaking. The rate used for discounting is r. Again, r represents the cost of capital. As we now know how to establish the cost of capital, r can be replaced by WACC. Hence, as shown in Equation 6.13, the complete formula to calculate NPV is:

$$
NPV = \left(FCF_0\right) + \frac{FCF_1}{(1+WACC)} + \frac{FCF_2}{(1+WACC)^2}
$$
$$
+ \frac{FCF_3}{(1+WACC)^3} + \cdots
$$

(6.13)

Any company wanting to create more value can either increase the future FCF and/or decrease the WACC (and this is why it is in the interest of the company to minimise its costs of equity and debt). In addition, if the cost of capital is lowered, there are potentially more positive NPV opportunities available, as some previously negative NPV projects may turn positive.

SUMMARY

Establishing the cost of equity entails estimating the rate of return required by shareholders. Two main methods have been reviewed here: the dividend growth model and CAPM. This chapter has also brought the previous discussion together, showing how to combine the costs of debt and equity to derive the WACC of a business. This WACC is then used to discount all the FCF in assessing an investment, following Equation 6.12.

This book has, so far, been devoted to explaining the components and makeup of various methods of evaluating investments. Yet, investments and projects are not just about buying new factories or equipment, or opening up new mines. To many businesses, investment opportunities also come in the form of buying other businesses. This is known as *mergers and acquisitions* (M&A), which is the focus of the two chapters that follow.

APPENDIX: CALCULATING THE COST OF CAPITAL – MC PRODUCTION, INC.

MC Production, Inc., as featured in the appendix of Chapter 3, is assessing a new project. Let's explore how its cost of capital is estimated. First things first, the company has a beta of 1.2. The return on the risk-free investment and the market return are 3 per cent and 8 per cent, respectively. The company has also issued a 4-year bond of £100,000 that offers a coupon rate of 5 per cent, with a face value of £121,000. The company is 70 per cent financed by equity, and the remainder is financed by the bond. All of these elements are shown in Figure 6.1A.

Cost of the bond

In order to calculate the cost of using the bond, it is necessary to establish the yield to maturity of the bond issued. This is illustrated in Equation 6.1A.

$$£100,000 = \frac{£5,000}{(1+YTM)} + \frac{£5,000}{(1+YTM)^2} + \frac{£5,000}{(1+YTM)^3} + \frac{£5,000 + £121,400}{(1+YTM)^4} \tag{6.1A}$$

The resulting YTM is 9.64 per cent.

A) Assumptions

Revenue in year 1	£	100,000	Beta		1.2
Growth in sales in each subsequent year		5%	Risk-free rate		3%
COGS in year 1	£	40,000	Market return		10%
Growth in COGS in each subsequent year		3%	Bond price at issue	£	100,000
SG&A in year 1	£	15,000	Face value	£	121,400
Growth in SG&A in each subsequent year		2%	Coupon rate		5%
Tax rate		30%	Maturity		4 years
Equipment (to be purchased in year 0)	£	160,000	Equity		70%
Depreciation method		Straight-line	Debt		30%
Length of the project		5 years			
NWC as a percentage of revenues next year		20%			
Cost of capital		10%			

B) Income Statement

	0	1	2	3	4	5
Revenue	£	100,000 £	105,000 £	110,250 £	115,763 £	121,551
COGS		(40,000)	(41,200)	(42,436)	(43,709)	(45,020)
Gross profit		60,000	63,800	67,814	72,053	76,530
SG&A		(15,000)	(15,300)	(15,606)	(15,918)	(16,236)
EBITDA		**45,000**	**48,500**	**52,208**	**56,135**	**60,294**
Depreciation		(32,000)	(32,000)	(32,000)	(32,000)	(32,000)
EBIT	£	**13,000 £**	**16,500 £**	**20,208 £**	**24,135 £**	**28,294**

C) Free Cash Flows Calculation

	0	1	2	3	4	5
1) CFO						
NOPAT	£	9,100 £	11,550 £	14,146 £	16,895 £	19,806
Depreciation		32,000	32,000	32,000	32,000	32,000
CFO	£	**41,100 £**	**43,550 £**	**46,146 £**	**48,895 £**	**51,806**
2) CAPEX						
+ CAPEX	£ (160,000)					
3) NWC						
NWC		20,000	21,000	22,050	23,153	24,310
+ Change in NWC	£ (20,000) £	(1,000) £	(1,050) £	(1,103) £	(1,158) £	24,310
FCF	£ (180,000) £	**40,100 £**	**42,500 £**	**45,043 £**	**47,737 £**	**76,116**
Discounted FCF	(180,000)	36,455	35,124	33,842	32,605	47,262
NPV	£ **5,287**					
IRR	**11.03%**					

Note: Brackets denote that it is a spending/an outflow of money

Figure 6.1A MC Production's project with financing details

Cost of equity

The cost of equity is estimated using CAPM, as shown in Equation 6.2A.

$$r_E = 3\% + 1.2 \ (10\% + 3\%) \tag{6.2A}$$

The cost of equity for MC Production is 11.4 per cent.

WACC and FCF discounting

Bringing both Equation 6.1A and Equation 6.2A together using the WACC method mentioned in Chapter 6 gives MC Production a cost of capital of 10 per cent.

$$WACC = 70\% \times 11.4\% + 30\% \times 9.64\% \times (1 - 30\%) \qquad (6.3A)$$

Finally, using the WACC to discount FCF generated by the project, we obtain an NPV of £5,287 and an IRR of 11.03 per cent. As the NPV is greater than 0 – supported by the fact that the IRR is greater than the WACC – the project is worth moving forward.

7

MERGERS AND ACQUISITIONS (I)

CHAPTER OVERVIEW

It is not uncommon that, during the course of their career, corporate employees will witness or participate in an acquisition of another business by their employer, or vice versa. Such buying and selling of companies is not restricted to large businesses snapping up smaller ones; very often, giant corporations do the same to each other.

This chapter and the next one will address key questions relating to mergers and acquisitions (M&A): what are the strategic, economic and financial reasons for buying or selling a company? What can the buyers and sellers gain from these takeover activities? How does taking over another business work? This chapter goes through the terminology, describes the most frequent types of M&A and examines the main motives behind them.

TERMINOLOGY

Many terms are used to refer to M&A, such as takeovers, mergers, acquisitions, buyouts, leverage buyouts, private equity and venture capital. Even though there is no hard-and-fast definition of these terms, how businesses and the media use them is often in reference to certain common characteristics.

Takeover

This term quite simply means that a company is seizing ownership of another company, paying for it and taking full control. Sometimes, the acquired business (often called the *target company*) becomes an integral part of the buyer (also called the *acquirer* or *bidder*). On other occasions, the acquired company retains its operational autonomy. In either case, its ownership is transferred to the acquirer. The term "takeover" is therefore often used as a synonym for M&A.

Merger

A merger takes place when two companies integrate with each other and become a (new) single entity. In particular, the term "merger" is frequently used in the context of the business combination of two large companies – hence the term "merger of equals", which can be represented by A + B = AB. The problem with the term "merger", however, is that, even when two businesses come together as one, there has to be a buyer and there has to be a seller. The term does not reveal much about which of the two companies is the new owner that assumes control of the resulting (newly created) entity.

Acquisition

Unlike "merger", this term generally suggests that a large company buys a smaller one ($A + b = A$), although this does not always have to be the case. The term is also used to describe a company buying another company of similar size, with which it integrates to form a bigger business ($a + b = A$). In this sense, this is more akin to the term "takeover". So, whereas with "acquisition" the role of each company involved is clear (one takes control of the other), the term does not technically provide direct hints about the relative size of the acquiring and acquired companies.

Mergers and acquisitions

This is a combination of the previous two terms. Given the fact that M&A encompasses all types of business combinations, this is the term businesses and the media generally use to describe the activities of buying and selling companies.

Buyout

This term refers to a highly specific company event – when the employees of a company buy the employing company from the current owner. There are many reasons why the employees could be interested in buying out the company that they are working for. One is that they believe that the owner(s) is not fully realising the company's potential. By assuming ownership, these managers can take the company further to create more value. Another reason is that the managers may see the employing company as wilting. As a way of saving the business and keeping their jobs, they may decide to take ownership of it.

Leverage buyout and private equity

As discussed in Chapter 5, leverage describes the use of debt to boost the return on equity. As the name suggests, leverage buyout (LBO) refers to the use of debt instruments to assist the managers in taking control and ownership of the company that they are working for. As a result of a number of scandals in the 1970s and 1980s related to LBOs, LBO companies now often refer to themselves as private equity (PE) firms.

A characteristic of a company that has gone through an LBO is that it will have a great deal of debt on its balance sheet and can therefore expect to make considerable interest payments. To service these payments, the company has to ensure that it performs well and reaches an earnings before interest and taxes (EBIT) that is large enough to cover the interest to be paid.

LBO/PE firms raise money from various investors to supply the equity needed for managers to buy out a business, supplemented with a huge proportion of debt. Very often, the company bought out is partially owned by the managers and partially by the PE firm. In order to make sure that the acquired company is in a position to pay the sizable interest, the PE firm further provides various kinds of assistance – such as board representation, technical and management expertise, potential customers and supplier networks – to help the acquired company grow. Given that PE firms rely heavily on debt to fund their buyouts, they tend to acquire businesses that have stable EBIT and cash flows. Consequently, mature companies or businesses in mature sectors with more predictable profitability and cash availability are of greater appeal to PE firms.

Venture capital

Like PE firms, venture capital (VC) firms raise money from various investors for equity injection into acquisitions. But, unlike PE firms, VC firms focus on investing in start-ups – fledgling companies that are at the early growth stage. In this case, VC firms tend to refrain from using debt because fledgling businesses are likely to have unpredictable and fluctuating EBIT (if they have positive EBIT at all!). Unpredictable EBIT means that it could be difficult to meet the interest payments needed. In addition, start-ups tend to have few tangible assets and therefore cannot use these to back their borrowing collaterals. As a result, VC firms almost always use equity to finance their purchases.

ALTERNATIVES TO M&A

One fundamental rationale underpins all types of acquisitions: companies buy other companies to grow their businesses and expand in size. Of course, M&A are not the only available growth strategy; companies have other options to augment themselves. Here are a few of them.

Organic growth or "greenfield"

This involves building and expanding the assets and operations of a business from scratch through business operations – in other words, building rather than buying.

Strategic alliances

Another growth option is to forge a partnership(s) between two (or more) companies whose assets and capabilities can complement each other. Often, the strategic partner is a competitor or a company in stage before or after in the value chain. Strategic alliances can aim for different degrees of collaboration, from partnership agreements to joint ventures. Think, for example, of airline companies belonging to alliance groups through which they can share their flights (i.e. codeshare) – this saves them from competing with each other and avoids partially filled planes. At the other end of the strategic alliance spectrum is the joint venture, in which two companies typically decide to set up a new entity and agree how they will both support it and what resources they will commit to it.

Naturally, there are pros and cons to each of these growth strategies, some of which are listed in Table 7.1.

Table 7.1 Advantages and disadvantages of various types of growth strategy for a business

	Advantages	*Disadvantages*
Organic growth	Company: • Has full control over its operations and decisions • Establishes operating routines and strategic directions with greater ease	Company: • Needs time (sometimes a lot of it) to build up the capabilities • Bears the full cost and risk of the investment
Strategic alliance	Company: • Benefits from local partners' knowledge and market power/positioning • Shares costs and risks with partners	Company: • Holds less control over the decisions regarding operating routines and strategic direction • Faces potential conflict as a result of shared ownership • Risks giving control of technology to partners (joint venture)
M&A	Acquiring company: • Achieves speed of building up the desired capabilities • Has tight control of operations • Pre-empts competitors by getting to the target first • Has no risk of losing technical competence to a competitor	Acquiring company: • Risks attaining disappointing results or over-optimistic expectations (in the event of poor integration) • May overpay for the target • Faces a culture clash between the two merging companies • May face obstacles to realise the expected synergies

FORMATS OF M&A

M&A can largely be categorised into three formats. The two most common types are horizontal and vertical integration. *Horizontal integration* refers to the acquisition of, or merger with, an industry competitor, with the aim of achieving the competitive advantages that come with being a large(r) operation.

By contrast, *vertical integration* refers to the purchase of a firm in the stage before or after in the value or supply chain. Such integration can be backwards (upstream), i.e. buying a company that produces the inputs for the acquirer, or forwards (downstream), i.e. the purchase of a company that the acquirer uses to distribute its products. A car manufacturer buying a car parts maker is an example of an upstream integration. A pharmaceutical wholesaler buying a high-street chemist chain is an example of integrating downstream.

Less common today is the third type of M&A called a *conglomerate*. This refers to acquiring companies in lines of business that are unrelated to those of the buyer, i.e. outside of the acquirer's value or supply chain.

M&A APPROACHES

A buyer initiates a merger or acquisition through a friendly or hostile approach. In a friendly M&A, the takeover is supported by the management of the target company. In this case, the management team of the selling company recommends that the shareholders relinquish ownership of the company by accepting the offer from the buyer. Even with this recommendation, the buyer must make an attractive offer that can persuade the target's shareholders to let go of their shares. To do so, a premium must be offered to them. *Acquisition premium* refers to the extra money that a buyer must pay, over and above the current share price, to entice the current shareholders to sell.

In contrast to friendly M&A, buyers can also take a hostile approach to the target, in which the bid goes against the wishes of the target company's management. The buying company will therefore have to make a direct offer to persuade the shareholders to sell, without the support of the management team. Making such a direct bid is often called a *tender offer*.

As can be imagined in this case, the management team puts up as much resistance as possible to frustrate the bid. The target leadership team can make it more difficult by restricting the would-be buyer's access to information. This can come in the form of disallowing the potential acquirer to conduct any *due diligence*. Due diligence in the M&A context refers to the process through which the buyer can evaluate a target company and its assets in person and not just on the basis of publicly available information. This is equivalent to putting the acquirer in a situation of buying a car without being able to kick the tyre, look beneath the bonnet and take it out for a test drive. By denying the option of due diligence, the buyer is likely to be ill-informed and, therefore, less able to establish the true value of the company. This places the buyer at risk of overpaying for the acquisition and, hence, can dissuade them from making the bid in the first place.

A less common M&A approach is the *reverse takeover*. This refers to the situation whereby, officially, company A buys company b, but, in reality, it is b that is paying for and owning A. This arrangement is sometimes necessary because of the sensitive nature of the transaction. For instance, if company A (a reputable and large national champion) is about to be gobbled up by company b (a smaller and lesser known company originating from a foreign country), A's government may oppose the deal. Therefore, in order to make the takeover acceptable to the government, the transaction can be structured and pitched as A buying b, even though the exact reverse is occurring. In this case, the combined business is likely to be called "A" or "Ab" to preserve A's image.

RATIONALE BEHIND M&A

When a company considers taking over another company, there are generally five sorts of motivations:

1   Operational
2   Industry-specific
3   Strategic
4   Financial
5   Personal

Two important points must be highlighted before delving deeper into these categories. First, a buyer may be using a combination of these motivations to rationalise their intention and grounds for the acquisition. Second, these motivations, or their combination, often lead to strategies that enable the merging entities to attain what is called *synergy*. Synergy occurs when two firms working together can produce an effect, benefits and gains that are larger than the sum of what they can achieve separately. A common representation of synergy is "1 + 1 = 3". A classic example of synergy is when, as two companies merge, the new entity can eliminate one of the human resources departments and hence "get more done with less".

1) Operational

Corporate decisions are often driven by the objective to improve the efficiency and effectiveness of the business. M&A help companies to do so through:

Achieving economies of scale

The term *economies of scale* refers to the cost advantage that arises when the outputs of a product increase without having increased the inputs. By buying another company to form a larger entity, the acquirer aims to produce a greater quantity of a good while lowering the costs on a per-unit basis. These costs are now spread across a higher volume of that one good. For instance, a company can negotiate a (better) discount when buying supplies in bulk. Another example is that, if a company can produce a bigger volume of output with just one machine, the cost of this piece of equipment can be spread across more products, making the cost of the products on a per-unit basis lower.

Attaining economies of scope

If economies of scale are about reducing costs over a larger number of the same goods sold, *economies of scope* refer to spreading the costs over a larger number of different goods. In practice, it is about lowering costs by sharing resources across businesses or a range of products. For example, when a major retail bank buys an insurance company in order to sell insurance policies to its existing and extensive base of bank customers, it is hoping to achieve economies of scope.

2) Industry-specific

Firms often engage in M&A to capitalise on various sector conditions or expand their capabilities to operate within their industries. Such industry-specific reasons include:

Increasing bargaining power

Becoming a larger company is associated with greater bargaining power over suppliers. A sizeable and more powerful company can also have more room for negotiation with its customers. In both cases, M&A enable a firm to increase its profitability at the expense of the other players in its value chain.

Building barriers to entry

Gaining control over the source of critical inputs or distribution channels can weaken rival companies and even stop potential competitors from entering the market. This is particularly the case if a firm acquires a rare resource or a company that has access to a rare resource.

Capturing the last opportunities

In some industries, there can be only a few major players. One of them may consider buying another because it can represent the last opportunity to grow through M&A. For instance, let's say there are five major supermarket chains in a market. If the government believes that there can be no fewer than four supermarket chains competing in the grocery retail market in order to protect consumers, for one of the five supermarket chains buying another, it represents the last chance to gain size and market share swiftly.

Managing industry rivalry

A company buying a rival reduces the number of competitors within an industry. One possible aim is to create price co-ordination, thereby preventing a price war that could erode the profit margin of every company in the industry. This is a particularly valid arrangement when there are only a few players in the market. Companies with a larger market share (as a result of M&A) could find it easier to co-ordinate with other big players to keep the prices high. It must be noted that, in many countries, it is legally forbidden to collude on price. Therefore, such price co-ordination can only be achieved tacitly, which requires the other players to understand the signals and be willing to collaborate.

3) Strategic

In addition to operational enhancements, firms buy others in order to strengthen their future revenue-generating abilities by:

Adding new resources

Companies can gain access to resources that were previously owned by other businesses. These resources can involve tangible assets, such as special machinery, equipment or store locations, and intangible assets, including patents, licences, reputation/brand name and operational expertise/processes. M&A allow for acquiring the human assets that possess the skills, commitment, knowledge and creativity that are essential in industries like professional services.

Increasing the value of products

A company can increase the value of its product offerings by bundling other products together with its own, adding new features or creating new offerings altogether. This often involves the acquisition of complementary products, which, in turn, enables the buyer to have full control over the integration of these products and the development of new ones.

Entering new markets

Buying or merging with a foreign company can enable the acquirer to gain speed in entering a new geographical market. In addition, a company that acquires a business can access a new customer segment, thereby creating new market spaces.

4) Financial

A firm can also merge with, or acquire, another to gain various financial advantages, including:

Exercising corporate governance

A company can seize control of a weak-performing firm and disband its management team. This is especially the case for LBO/PE firms. PE firms take full control of underperforming/undervalued businesses, turning them around and making them profitable again. By restoring the acquired firm in order to fulfil its potential, the buyer can create value for its shareholders.

Diversifying risk

Some buyers in the past have argued and reasoned that acquiring other businesses can help diversify the risk of their portfolios, which, in turn, lowers the risk for their shareholders. This is arguably a tenuous rationale. The reason is that, as explained in the previous chapter, shareholders can lower the risk themselves by holding a well-diversified portfolio. Why do they need the company to engage in very expensive M&A activities when they can achieve similar results cheaply and easily by diversifying their own investment portfolios?

Increasing debt capacity

In theory at least, buying a firm that has little debt can potentially expand the buyer's capacity to borrow. Similarly, acquiring another firm with stable and predictable cash flows and EBIT can help the buyer to take on more debt, as the additional stable income makes it more able to meet the interest payments.

Improving the earnings per share

One of the more popular financial reasons for M&A involves improving the buyer's earnings per share (EPS). EPS is calculated by dividing the company's net income by the number of shares outstanding. Effectively, it represents the proportion of net profit that a company has made in a year and that each share is entitled to. If, after the M&A, the EPS of the (now bigger) buyer increases, then the transaction is EPS accretive. If the EPS drops, it is called dilutive. An accretive M&A transaction may, by itself, be insufficient as a reason for the takeover. However, it can be a powerful additional (financial) reason for the transaction to take place.

5) Personal

Last but not least, some managers conduct M&A for the purpose of making personal gains. Running a larger company is often akin to having greater prestige. Some acquisition-inclined CEOs are driven by empire-building behaviour and/or want to make their firms larger and more dominant. This not only brings higher status, but perhaps also satisfies managerial ego. Additionally, a larger business can provide a reason to get an upward revision of the salaries of the executives.

SUMMARY

This chapter has examined the terminology and buzzwords commonly used in the area of M&A. It has looked at alternative types of partnerships than M&A, as well as the format of and approaches to takeover activities. Five main rationales for company acquisition have also been covered here. Whereas this chapter has concentrated on the strategic perspectives of an acquisition, the next chapter delves into the financial side of M&A and business valuation.

8

MERGERS AND ACQUISITIONS (II)

CHAPTER OVERVIEW

The previous chapter examined the types and drivers of mergers and acquisitions (M&A). This chapter focuses on how to value a business in order for the buyer to determine the price (and for the seller to decide at what price to sell it). While considerable literature exists on the traditional valuation methods, professionals often modify and tailor them to fit their own needs and requirements. Consequently, there is no single standard. This chapter provides an overview of the fundamentals of company valuation, with the aim of giving the readers an understanding of the main methods and the rationale behind them.

HOW CAN A COMPANY BE VALUED?

Unlike shopping in a store, there is no price tag dangling out of a company. Nor is it possible to use a cost-based approach. Unlike in a situation where a manufacturer can decide on the price of a product based on the cost of the materials, labour and production, and the required profit margin, it is hard to determine the value of a company in the absence of similar parameters.

It is not uncommon to believe that a company is worth what it owns, i.e. it is the sum of its tangible and intangible assets. Put differently, if a company has £100 million in assets, according to this view it must mean that the company itself is worth £100 million.

However, this view is wrong for several reasons:

1   While it may be easy to calculate how much the tangible assets, such as buildings and equipment, are currently worth – and

hence their market value – it is often much more difficult to place a value on intangible assets, like intellectual property and brand. Hence, the value of the assets the company owns is a poor indicator of how much it is worth.

2   There are value-creating factors that a company may use but that are not captured on the balance sheet. These factors include human resources, processes, knowledge, practices, customers, client networks and location advantages. Imagine buying a law firm. Office buildings, furniture and IT equipment will appear on its balance sheet (if the target company is not renting them). Does that mean the law firm is only worth these items? Probably not. It is likely that the buyer of the firm is far more interested in the target's capabilities to make money than in the building, furniture and IT equipment. Yet, such capabilities are not reflected on the balance sheet.

3   While purchasing another business can increase the size of the buyer and its assets, the buyer is mostly interested in the possible synergistic gains for the combined business. However, the worth of the target's assets does not reflect such gains.

All these reasons point to a key principle in valuation: the worth of a company is not based on the value of the assets on its balance sheet. Instead, it is based on how much value the company can create with its assets. This means that it is much better to value a business by measuring the free cash flows (FCF) that it can generate in the future, in the same way as investments and projects are assessed.

FCF-based balance sheet

Let's start by looking at the FCF through the lens of the balance sheet. Figure 8.1a displays a conventional balance sheet, similar to the one that has been used throughout this book. Figure 8.1b, on the other hand, shows a different balance sheet, with items from the perspective of cash flows. It is necessary to note that it is *not* a common practice to create balance sheet based on FCF. Yet, this is very helpful in illustrating the fundamentals of company valuation.

Focusing on figure b, A) represents the FCF that can be generated by the company's fixed assets (made up of cash flows from operations (CFO) and capital expenditure (CAPEX)) discounted in

| | 8.1a | | 8.1b | |

Traditional balance sheet   **FCF-based balance sheet**

Assets	Total liabilities and shareholders' equity	"Assets"	"Total liabilities and shareholders' equity"
Current assets	Current liabilities	B) PV of cash flows from NWC	D) Market value of long-term debt
Fixed assets	Long-term debt	A) PV of cash flows from fixed assets (i.e. CFO and CAPEX)	C) Market value of shareholders' equity
	Shareholders' equity		
Total assets	Total liabilities and shareholders' equity	PV of all the FCF of the company	Total market value of long-term debt and shareholders' equity

Figure 8.1 Traditional vs. FCF-based balance sheet

today's terms. Effectively, this is the present value (PV) of all the cash flows that the fixed assets can generate.

B), on the other hand, requires more explanation. It focuses on net working capital (NWC) – the third ingredient in FCF. Recall that NWC is the result of subtracting current liabilities from current assets. Hence, the current liabilities item that traditionally sits on the right-hand side of the balance sheet is "moved" to the left-hand side, forming the NWC. Again, like A), B) shows the PV of all future cash flows related to the NWC.

C) and D) on the right-hand side of Figure 8.1b, like the traditional accounting system, are related to how the assets are financed. Just like the left-hand side, where both the NWC and fixed assets are in PV terms, it is necessary to establish the current value of both long-term debt and equity. But how do we estimate such values?

Let's start with C), the current value of equity – i.e. how investors price the shares today. For large companies that are publicly traded, this is fairly easy to establish as this is based on the current share price – the price at which the shares are trading on the stock market today. It is, however, very difficult (if not impossible) to establish the share price of private companies. In this case, it involves getting professionals, such as accountants, to conduct analyses and make some assumptions. For the purpose of illustrating the concept, let's stick to publicly traded businesses.

To figure out the shareholders' equity in current value, we need to calculate the so-called *market capitalisation*. As displayed in

Equation 8.1, market capitalisation is the number of shares that are currently traded multiplied by the current share price.

$$\text{Market capitalisation} = \text{Number of shares outstanding} \times \text{Share price} \tag{8.1}$$

While many people have heard of this term, some confuse it with the value of a company. This *could* be the case, provided the company has no debt. However, if the company is financed by both debt and equity, the market capitalisation is only reflecting the equity side of the business, i.e. the part of the business that belongs to shareholders. In this case, it is necessary to also take into account the part of the business financed by debt.

Therefore, to determine the value of the business as a whole, we must establish the market value of the debt − D) in Figure 8.1b. However, this may be difficult given that, unlike shares, debt is mostly private. Granted, some bonds are traded in the market, which enables analysts to calculate their market value, but they represent only a small proportion of the total amount of debt in the market. Furthermore, information on privately arranged debts and loans is often confidential. As a result of lacking such information, in practice, people tend to use book value, i.e. the actual amount that a company borrowed when the debt was taken on. Adding C) and D) together leads to the total market value of long-term debt and shareholders' equity. Since a balance sheet must balance, the total PV of all FCF must be equal to the total market value of long-term debt and shareholders' equity.

The "FCF-based" balance sheet shows us that there is not just one way, but two ways, to establish the value of a company:

1   The left-hand side of Figure 8.1b is effectively valuing the company from an *internal* perspective. This is because we are looking at how much cash flows a company can generate in the future using all of what it has.
2   The right-hand side, by contrast, focuses on the *external* aspect of the company. This suggests that, by establishing how the investors view and value a company's debt and equity, it is possible to figure out how much the market would value the business.

In turn, these two viewpoints form the basis of the three most common valuation methods.

THE THREE MOST COMMON VALUATION METHODS

There are three main methods to value companies. Even though different people may use their own versions and variations of these approaches, the central principle and mechanism remain the same. These methods are 1) the weighted average cost of capital (WACC) method, 2) industry comparables and 3) M&A comparables.

1) WACC method

The basis for this method is simple. It centres around calculating the PV of the company, because this is how much value it is expected to create in the future. The PV is calculated by projecting and estimating all the company's FCF from the following year onwards and then discounting them with the WACC.

The first step of the method is to divide the company's future timeline into two parts: 1) the explicit forecast period and 2) the terminal value. As an example, to forecast the FCF of Company Bob, it is possible to divide the time period as shown in Figure 8.2.

Explicit forecast period

In this example, the explicit forecast period spans the next 8 years. As the name suggests, this is the time period over which the FCF are projected through detailed analyses. Recall that the FCF are made up of CFO, CAPEX and change in NWC, so the assumptions on all revenues and costs, investment expenditure and the working capital as a result of the acquisition are examined closely in order to estimate the benefits that can be extracted from the M&A.

Explicit forecast period								Terminal value
0	1	2	3	4	5	6	7	8	9 and beyond
	FCF_1	FCF_2	FCF_3	FCF_4	FCF_5	FCF_6	FCF_7	FCF_8	TV

Figure 8.2 An example of an explicit forecast period and terminal value

For instance, if Company Alice intends to buy Company Bob, Alice will include in the FCF forecast of Bob the synergistic gains it expects to create. Synergies were defined in the previous chapter as the ability to achieve larger gains as one entity than the sum of the gains of each separate company. Alice must therefore estimate the synergistic effects additional benefits of the acquisition on the projected sales and costs, on the working capital requirements and on the additional CAPEX required in the explicit forecast period of the combined entity. All of these in turn form the FCF in each of the coming 8 years for Bob.

The logic behind the explicit forecast period implies that all the gains to be attained from acquiring Bob will take place in the first 8 years. How is this (optimal) forecast period determined? The answer lies in the concept of competitive advantage. Competitive advantage refers to an edge that enables a company to earn above industry average profit. However, such advantage is not everlasting; over time, products and services become obsolete, innovations get copied and novelty wears off. Therefore, in all cases, competitive advantage gradually disappears. In this example, Alice expects to lose, over the next 8 years, the competitive advantage that it can gain from acquiring Bob.

But what determines the length of the explicit forecast period? The answer is that it depends on the nature of the industries. For example, a power generation business may hold onto its advantage longer than other types of business due to the high barrier to get into this mature and expensive-to-enter industry. Contrast this to a computer component manufacturer that operates in a highly competitive market. Many of the advantages gained from an acquisition of such a company may vanish in a matter of a few years, as rival firms can catch up fast. In this case, a much shorter explicit forecast period would be used.

Terminal value

This discussion on competitive advantage points to a common misunderstanding: that a company with no competitive advantage is doomed. This is not the case at all. If having a competitive advantage is to be able to earn above-average profit, then not possessing such advantage simply means that the company is earning industry average profit. Extending this logic, as long as a company holds a (certain) share of a market and that the market is growing ever so slightly, it can still expect profitability over a long period of time. Indeed, even if a company is not getting a bigger share of the pie, it will benefit as a result of the pie becoming larger. This idea underpins the concept of *terminal value*.

Terminal value (hereafter TV) refers to the PV of all the FCF in infinite future years, starting at the end of the explicit forecast period. Given that the TV includes/incorporates all the future FCF generated forever, it is possible to draw on the growing perpetuity formula introduced in Chapter 2, which is repeated in Equation 8.2, where PV is the present value, C_1 next year's cash flow, r the discount rate and g the growth rate.

$$PV = \frac{C_1}{r - g} \tag{8.2}$$

Applying this to the concept of TV, it will become what is shown in Equation 8.3, where WACC refers to the weighted average cost of capital.

$$TV_0 = \frac{FCF_1}{WACC - g} \tag{8.3}$$

In the case of Company Bob, since it has an 8-year explicit forecast period, the TV will only start in year 9. The formula for TV thus needs to be adjusted for the correct time period. This is shown in Equation 8.4.

$$TV_8 = \frac{FCF_9}{WACC - g} \tag{8.4}$$

Given that Bob is expected to grow at a constant rate of g every year (meaning that it is only going to make industry average gains from this point onwards), the FCF in year 9 must be the year 8 FCF increased by this growth rate. Equation 8.4 can therefore be written as Equation 8.5.

$$TV_8 = \frac{FCF_8 \times (1 + g)}{WACC - g} \tag{8.5}$$

The g used in these equations refers to the average growth rate of the industry over time. Even though, in practice, professionals have different ways of establishing the growth rate, many use the GDP growth rate as a proxy. The assumption behind this is that, as long as the economy is growing, the industry should be growing accordingly. Admittedly, this is a crude assumption, as, for instance, a declining industry does not grow when the economy expands. Yet, for companies operating in a stable industry setting, this assumption may have merit. A popular alternative proxy is the expected rate of inflation. The idea is simple: as long as there is inflation, revenues and costs grow. Ultimately, however, there is no right or wrong answer as to the level of g, and determining it is a subjective decision. The resulting FCF from the explicit forecast period and the TV estimation are shown in Figure 8.3, where FCF_9 is equal to $FCF_8 \times (1 + g)$.

WACC

The next step is to estimate the WACC. Using the cost of capital of the buyer may come to mind. This makes sense because, in order to be value-creating, the acquisition needs to satisfy the return required by the acquirer's debt and equity investors. There are, however, exceptions. What happens if Alice decides to have a different capital structure for Bob than its own? For example, Alice can get Bob to take up a lot of debt to finance the deal, which would make it end up with a very different cost of capital from that of Alice. In such a case, to value Bob, both the FCF and TV should be discounted by Bob's WACC, since it takes into account how much debt and equity Alice wants Bob to have.

The value of the firm can now be derived by discounting all the future FCF and the TV with the WACC, as shown in Equation 8.6. The result (being the value of the firm) is known as the *enterprise value*, or simply EV.

$$
EV = \frac{FCF_1}{(1+WACC)} + \frac{FCF_2}{(1+WACC)^2} + \frac{FCF_3}{(1+WACC)^3} \\
+ \cdots \frac{FCF_8 + TV_8}{(1+WACC)^8}
\tag{8.6}
$$

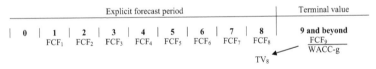

Figure 8.3 FCF from the explicit forecast period and terminal value

Example of the WACC method

Figure 8.4 provides an illustration of how the WACC valuation method works. It starts with Bob's projected income statement, factoring in all the synergistic gains in both revenues and costs, in the 8 years of the explicit forecast period. The resulting annual earnings before interest and taxes (EBIT) are then fed into the calculation

A) Assumptions

Tax rate	35.0%
Growth rate	4.0%
WACC	10.0%

B) Income statement

(in £ millions unless otherwise stated)

	0	1	2	3	4	5	6	7	8	9 and beyond
				Explicit forecast period						Terminal value
Revenue		£ 30.0	£ 33.0	£ 36.3	£ 39.9	£ 43.9	£ 48.3	£ 53.1	£ 58.5	
COGS		(14.0)	(15.1)	(16.3)	(17.6)	(19.0)	(20.6)	(22.2)	(24.0)	
Gross profit		16.0	17.9	20.0	22.3	24.9	27.7	30.9	34.5	
SG&A		(5.0)	(5.4)	(5.8)	(6.3)	(6.8)	(7.3)	(7.9)	(8.6)	
EBITDA		11.0	12.5	14.1	16.0	18.1	20.4	23.0	25.9	
D & A		(2.0)	(2.0)	(2.0)	(2.0)	(2.0)	(2.0)	(2.0)	(2.0)	
EBIT		£ 9.0	£ 10.5	£ 12.1	£ 14.0	£ 16.1	£ 18.4	£ 21.0	£ 23.9	

C) Free cash flows calculation

(in £ millions unless otherwise stated)

	0	1	2	3	4	5	6	7	8	9 and beyond
				Explicit forecast period						
1) CFO										
NOPAT		£ 5.9	£ 6.8	£ 7.9	£ 9.1	£ 10.4	£ 12.0	£ 13.6	15.5	
Depreciation		2.0	2.0	2.0	2.0	2.0	2.0	2.0	2.0	
CFO		£ 7.9	£ 8.8	£ 9.9	£ 11.1	£ 12.4	£ 14.0	£ 15.6	£ 17.5	
2) CAPEX										
+ CAPEX		£ (6.0)	£ (6.0)	£ (6.0)	£ (6.0)	£ (6.0)	£ (6.0)	£ (6.0)	£ (6.0)	
3) Change in NWC										
+ Change in NWC		£ (2.0)	£ (2.0)	£ (2.0)	£ (2.0)	£ (2.0)	£ (2.0)	£ (2.0)	£ (2.0)	
FCF		£ (0.1)	£ 0.8	£ 1.9	£ 3.1	£ 4.4	£ 6.0	£ 7.6	£ 9.5	
Terminal value									£ 165.3	
Discounted FCF										
PV of FCF		£ (0.1)	£ 0.7	£ 1.4	£ 2.1	£ 2.8	£ 3.4	£ 3.9	£ 4.4	
Sum of PV of FCF	£ 18.6									
PV of terminal value	£ 77.1									
EV of Bob	£ 95.7									

Note: Brackets denote that it is a spending/an outflow of money

Figure 8.4 Example of the WACC method

of CFO in the FCF analysis. The projected CAPEX and additional working capital needed are also included in this analysis, in order to derive the FCF for all the years in the explicit forecast period.

The TV is based on the free cash flow in year 9, which is £9.5 million × (1 + 4% growth rate), or £9.9 million the year straight after the explicit forecast period. Applying this to Equation 8.4, the resulting TV of £165.3 million represents the PV of all the FCF from year 9 onwards. To bring it to today's value, this TV is discounted by (1 + the WACC of 10%),[8] arriving at £77.1 million. Adding this PV of the TV to the PV of all FCF from the first 8 years, the EV of Bob is found to be £95.7 million.

Valuation is about finding an EV range

Newcomers tend to subscribe to the view that the aim of company valuation is to produce one single EV. However, this is not the case at all. The goal of a valuation is, in fact, to come up with a *range* of values for the worth of a company.

Since the WACC method only yields one result, establishing a range of values involves conducting a *sensitivity analysis*. A sensitivity analysis is a technique that enables us to see how a change in the assumptions can alter the end result. In the current context, it means examining how the two inputs that can have the greatest impact – the WACC and the growth rate – affect the EV.

Figure 8.5 offers an example of a sensitivity analysis of Bob's EV by varying the growth rate (in the range of 2–6 per cent) and the WACC (in the range of 8–12 per cent). The general practice is to use a range between plus and minus 2 per cent. The analysis suggests that, given the range of assumptions made, Bob's value is between £56.0 million and £293.7 million.

(in £ millions unless otherwise stated)

		WACC				
		8.00%	9.00%	10.0%	11.00%	12.00%
Growth rate	2.00%	108.3	89.3	75.3	64.5	56.0
	3.00%	126.8	101.8	84.0	70.9	60.7
	4.00%	154.7	119.1	95.7	79.1	66.7
	5.00%	201.0	145.2	112.0	90.0	74.4
	6.00%	293.7	188.7	136.4	105.3	84.7

Figure 8.5 Sensitivity analysis of Bob's EV

So we end up with a wide value range. To narrow down this range, professionals often triangulate the WACC method with the industry comparables and M&A comparables. Let's now turn to the first of the two.

2) Industry comparables

Sometimes called *trading comparables*, the second valuation tool is industry comparables, or simply industry comps. This method estimates the value of a company by comparing it to that of its competitors. The starting point is to capture at least the revenue, earnings before interest, taxes, depreciation and amortisation (EBITDA) and the EBIT information of both the company being valued and its rival firms. The next step is to establish the EV of the competitors. Recall that, as in Figure 8.1b, EV can be estimated by totalling the market value of debt and equity. In other words, we can obtain the EV of each rival firm by adding up their respective current debt and equity values.

Based on this idea, the standard equation to do this is shown in Equation 8.7:

$$EV = Market\ capitalisation + Net\ debt + Minority\ interest \\ + Preferred\ shares \tag{8.7}$$

As discussed earlier, market capitalisation represents the market value of equity. Debt, on the other hand, is either the market value (if the information is available) or, if not available, simply the book value – the value at which the debt was first issued. So, by combining debt and equity, we can establish the EV of a company. Yet, it is necessary to make an adjustment by deducting cash from debt to calculate the company's value. The total debt less the amount of cash (i.e. total debt – cash) that a company has is called its *net debt*.

There are two ways of explaining why we have to do this. One is to think of cash as, effectively, *negative* debt: any cash that comes with the acquired company can be used to offset the purchase price, thereby lowering the price and value of the company. (If you pay £10 for a product that comes with a £2 coin, the actual purchase price and, thus, value of the product is £8.) Another way to think of cash is that, by itself, cash sitting in a bank account is an unproductive asset: it does not contribute to the value of the company because any value created comes from how the cash is invested, not its mere presence.

The calculation of EV also takes into account two fairly uncommon items: minority interest and preferred shares. Minority interest, or non-controlling interest, refers to the ownership of less than 50 per cent of a company's equity by an investor or another company. So, if Company ABC owns under 50 per cent of another business called DEF, this fraction of DEF is added to the value of ABC. After all, this small part of DEF belongs to ABC!

Preferred shares encompass a class of shares that are more senior than common shares but more junior than debt (hence, they sit between debt and common shares on the balance sheet). Since preferred shares are a part of the financing of the company, like debt and common equity, they should be included in the calculation of EV in Equation 8.7.

Comparing with rival firms

To illustrate, let's assume that Company Bob has four main competitors. Their current financial details are shown in Table 8.1. In real life, this information can typically be found in the most recent financial reports and market information. To keep matters simple, the calculation of these competitors' EVs excludes minority interest and preferred shares. The table also contains Bob's most recent revenues, EBITDA and EBIT.

The first step in the industry comps approach is to create a set of *multiples* out of the competitors' financials. This is achieved by dividing the competitors' EVs with their respective performance measures. The multiples calculated based on Table 8.1 are shown in Table 8.2.

Table 8.1 Current financials and EVs of Bob's competitors (in £ millions unless otherwise stated)

	Revenue	EBITDA	EBIT
Bob	£ 20.0	£ 8.0	£ 7.0

	Revenue	EBITDA	EBIT	Market cap.	Debt	Cash	Net debt (Debt − Cash)	EV (Market cap. + Net debt)
Rival 1	£12.0	£10.0	£7.0	£95.0	£15.0	£30.0	(£15.0)	£80.0
Rival 2	£16.0	£13.0	£9.0	£90.0	£70.0	£10.0	£60.0	£150.0
Rival 3	£8.0	£5.0	£2.0	£52.0	£4.0	£10.0	(£6.0)	£46.0
Rival 4	£31.0	£26.0	£23.0	£303.0	£63.0	£10.0	£53.0	£356.0

Table 8.2 Industry comps multiples of Bob's competitors

	EV/revenue	*EV/EBITDA*	*EV/EBIT*
Rival 1	6.7×	8.0×	11.4×
Rival 2	9.4×	11.5×	16.7×
Rival 3	5.8×	9.2×	23.0×
Rival 4	11.5×	13.7×	15.5×
Min.	5.8×	8.0×	11.4×
Max.	11.5×	13.7×	23.0×
Average	8.3×	10.6×	16.6×
Average (excluding outliers)	8.0×	10.4×	16.1×
Selected range	**6.0× – 12.0×**	**8.0× – 14.0×**	**12.0× – 18.0×**

For example, Rival 1's EV is £80.0 million and, after dividing it by its revenue of £12.0 million, the resulting EV/revenue multiple is 6.7×.

Calculating the multiples based on revenue, EBITDA and EBIT for each competitor allows us to determine a range of multiples based on the minimum and maximum multiples for each category.

There are two important points to make here. First, under EV/EBIT, Rival 3's multiple of 23.0× is much larger than the multiples of the other companies. In this case, it *might* be wise to treat it as an outlier, as its inclusion in the multiple could cause the value range to be overestimated. So, how can we decide whether a multiple is an outlier or not? Well, there is no hard-and-fast rule for this. It remains a *subjective* choice.

This leads to the second and perhaps most important point: how the range is chosen is often also a subjective decision. There are no formal rules or conventions on forming the criteria to determine the range of multiples. The criteria of such a range are often, in practice, informed by the opinions, views and experience of the professionals conducting the valuation.

Establishing Bob's EV through industry comps

The range of multiples created can then be used to establish Bob's value. For instance, the EV/revenue multiples of 6.00× and 12.00× are applied to Bob's revenue of £20.0 million. This suggests that Bob's EV based on this multiple is between £120.0 million and £240.0 million. The same process is repeated for the EBITDA and EBIT multiples, using Bob's EBITDA and EBIT. The results are shown in Table 8.3.

This exercise has shown the different possible values of the company. According to EV/EBITDA, Bob's value ranges somewhere between £64.0 million and £112.0 million, whereas with EV/EBIT the range is between £84.0 million and £126.0 million. However, there are pitfalls of the industry comps method that users should be aware of.

Table 8.3 Value of Bob based on the industry comps
(in £ millions unless otherwise stated)

	EV/revenue	*EV/EBITDA*	*EV/EBIT*
Rival 1	6.7×	8.0×	11.4×
Rival 2	9.4×	11.5×	16.7×
Rival 3	5.8×	9.2×	23.0×
Rival 4	11.5×	13.7×	15.5×
Min.	5.8×	8.0×	11.4×
Max.	11.5×	13.7×	23.0×
Average	8.3×	10.6×	16.6×
Average (excluding outliers)	8.0×	10.4×	16.1×
Selected range	6.0× – 12.0×	8.0× – 14.0×	12.0× – 18.0×

	Revenue	*EBITDA*	*EBIT*
Bob	£ 20.0	£ 8.0	£ 7.0

Range	*Bob's EV based on revenue*	*Bob's EV based on EBITDA*	*Bob's EV based on EBIT*
Lower end	£120.0	£64.0	£84.0
Higher end	£240.0	£112.0	£126.0

Pitfalls of the industry comps method

This valuation method, while popular, is far from flawless. Its main shortcoming lies in the selection of comparable firms. For instance, some companies effectively define their sectors/industries, which makes them unique. It could be hard to identify the close competitors to, say, Facebook, or even to pinpoint its exact industry. Pioneering companies, especially in high tech, may have no competitors. Indeed, even if a company operates in a precisely definable industry, finding comparable rival firms can still be challenging. Take, for example, the car-making industry. To value, say, the German luxury carmaker BMW using this method, either the public information needed for its competitors is unavailable (e.g. Mercedes-Benz is not traded on the stock market, only its parent company is) or their characteristics can be very different from those of BMW (e.g. should Porsche, a specialised sports car producer, or Toyota, a mass-market automobile manufacturer that also owns the luxury brand Lexus, be included in the comps?). Ultimately, the choice of companies that make up the comparable universe is subjective, i.e. it depends on one's own industry assessment.

3) M&A comparables

Also called *transaction comps*, the third method is to assess the M&A comparables (or simply M&A comps). Its principle is very similar to that of the industry comps method. The main difference is that, instead of basing the valuation on the current value of different rivals, this analysis uses information from historical M&A transactions in the target's industry (typically from the past 10 years) to establish the range of values. For the purpose of illustration, Table 8.4 provides a list of the M&A transactions in the last 10 years for the industry in which Bob operates.

The first step is to calculate the multiples using the transaction values – the amounts that the target companies were bought for – and the EBITDA of the target companies at the time when they were sold. So, according to the information here, 8 years ago, Company Cyan paid £180.0 million to buy Company Grey. At that time, Grey's EBITDA was £13.0 million, thus leading to an EBITDA multiple of 13.8× (£180.0 million ÷ £13.0 million).

However, this calculation is incorrect. This is because, in every acquisition, as discussed in the previous chapter, buyers have to pay an

Table 8.4 M&A comps in Bob's industry
(in £ millions unless otherwise stated)

Dates	Acquirer	Target	Transaction value	Implied company value	Target's EBITDA when purchased	EBITDA multiple
Year X–8	Cyan	Grey	£180.0	£138.5	£13.0	10.7×
Year X–5	Brown	Black	£200.0	£153.8	£23.0	6.7×
Year X–4	Blue	Orange	£44.7	£34.4	£4.0	8.6×
Year X–3	Red	Yellow	£80.0	£61.5	£8.0	7.7×
Year X–3	Green	Purple	£105.0	£80.8	£6.0	13.5×
Average						9.4×
Selected range						**7.0× – 13.0×**

acquisition premium to entice the shareholders of the target business to sell their shares. Usually, on large transactions, such a premium is well publicised. In smaller, private deals, on the other hand, it may not be disclosed. Yet, historical data suggest that, on average, the acquisition premium is 30 per cent, i.e. 30 per cent more than the value of the seller to the buyer. Hence, it is common practice to assume a 30 per cent premium for the purpose of calculating EV.

Thus, the *implied* company value of the acquired business, Grey, (excluding the acquisition premium) is estimated as: £180.0 million ÷ (1 + 30%) = £138.5 million. Using this implied company value and dividing it by the EBITDA of £13.0 million gives a corrected EBITDA multiple of 10.7× (£138.5 million ÷ £13.0 million). The same calculation is then repeated for all the transactions in the competitors' universe to reach the value range. Similarly to industry comps, the range of values is selected subjectively. Also, the opinion on whether an outlier, such as the multiple of 6.7× of the Brown/Black merger, should be included or not varies from one person to another.

Establishing the value of ABC through M&A comps

As shown in Table 8.5, just like industry comps, the EV of Bob is calculated by multiplying the corresponding number to the multiples.

Table 8.5 Bob's EV based on M&A comps
(in £ millions unless otherwise stated)

Range	EV based on EBITDA
Lower end	£56.0
Higher end	£104.0

Hence, multiplying Bob's EBITDA of £8.0 million by the range of 7.0× – 13.0× leads to an EV of £56.0 million to £104.0 million.

Pitfalls of the M&A comps method

One of the major problems with the M&A comps method is that there may be a limited number of relevant past transactions within an industry. Let's revisit the car-making industry. There would be very few, if any, M&A deals between automobile manufacturers in the past 10 years given that there is only a limited number of them in the world. Consequently, such an M&A comps universe would have to be broadened to include acquisitions in other segments of the car-making industry – for instance, the acquisition of car parts makers – even though their characteristics are different from those of car manufacturers in many respects. Given that the selection of the transactions can impact the valuation range significantly, it should be remembered that a great deal of bias is likely to be present in the M&A comps method.

PUTTING THE THREE APPROACHES TOGETHER

The findings from the three methods discussed in this chapter are placed alongside each other in Figure 8.6. The final range of EV for Bob is selected by making a judgement on the basis of all the analyses conducted along the way. In this case, £90.0 million to £140.0 million seems to be the most realistic EV value range.

But how is this final range of EV chosen? The answer is, again, through subjective judgement. It is up to the person conducting the valuation to decide what they think is the most likely range of values. It should be clear by now that arriving at the value of a company involves a substantial amount of subjective opinions, introducing personal biases along the way.

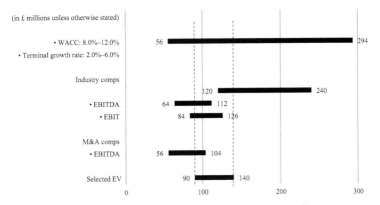

Figure 8.6 Establishing Bob's EV

IMPORTANT POINTS ABOUT COMPANY VALUATION

The fact that valuation is about finding a range of possible values based on a great deal of subjective personal judgements highlights a number of important lessons.

There is no single value of a company

Instead, there is a range of potential values. Valuation is not an exact science. Company valuation is not about pinpointing the precise value of a business. Rather, the ultimate aim of the valuation exercise is to establish an idea of what the company's value could be so as to facilitate further discussions and negotiations.

There are inherent biases

Each of the three methods involves different biases and assumptions. Consequently, they often lead to (very) different results. Hence, it is important to understand the implications of the various methods well in order to lead the negotiations in the preferred direction.

Parameters have impact

Technical parameters such as the WACC and the growth rate used in the WACC method have a great impact on the projected value. It is therefore paramount to allocate enough time to estimating them when conducting a valuation.

The final transaction value is likely to be different

The final purchase/sold value usually differs from the initially estimated value. This is because the subsequent negotiations and conversations, as well as the due diligence offer insights and information, can drastically change the assumptions of the valuation model. Valuation should therefore be an iterative exercise that incorporates additional information.

To sum up, ultimately, it is the quality of the analysis of the valuation that really counts. A valuation that takes into account realistic assumptions and informed projections and that captures as much quality information as possible is more likely to provide insights into how the acquired company will perform in the future. Ultimately, a significant portion of the transaction value – if not the whole transaction value – depends on the negotiation skills of the participants.

SUMMARY

This chapter has covered the fundamentals of company valuation. As the three most common valuation approaches reveal – the WACC method, industry comps and M&A comps – personal judgements, opinions and experience count as much as, if not more than, the financial analyses. This should not be a surprise because, ultimately, corporate finance is just a set of tools and techniques to help people make decisions. With the discussion on M&A in this chapter and those prior, we have covered all the necessary ground. The next chapter connects up all the ideas that this book has introduced.

CORPORATE FINANCE

The big picture

CHAPTER OVERVIEW

The aim of this book was to provide a clear understanding of the fundamentals of corporate finance. For many beginners, learning these fundamentals can be challenging. One of the major obstacles is the ability to see how the many concepts and themes introduced are connected to each other. Being able to grasp the relationships between the concepts can certainly help to reinforce an understanding of the underlying rationale behind them. This, in turn, often makes it easier to get a view of corporate finance as a whole. Figure 9.1 forms the core of the final chapter and is an original way of capturing all the topics covered in this book in one summarising picture, explicitly displaying the connections between them. The rest of the chapter offers a summary of the key topics outlined in the figure.

FROM ECONOMICS AND ACCOUNTING . . .

Corporate finance is about creating value for investors in a company, especially the shareholders. Some of the foundations of value creation originate from economics.

The subject of economics suggests that an individual or a company aims to reap the maximum benefit from investing their limited resources. These resources, from the corporate perspective, often include employees, buildings and machines. Yet, the one single most important resource for hiring people and buying equipment is capital, which is at the centre of corporate finance. Therefore, corporate finance represents concepts and tools that help managers make money

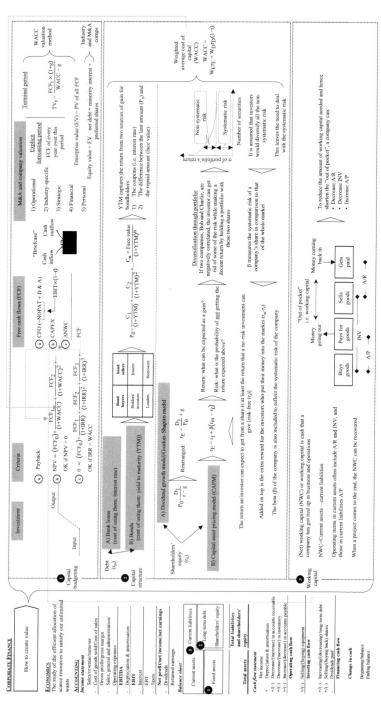

Figure 9.1 Corporate finance: the big picture

and generate a return for the investors, namely those who injected capital in the business.

To generate a return for the investors, managers have to improve and expand the company's operations. This is why the accounting financial statements play such an important role in corporate finance. These accounting statements portray the historical and current performance, as well as the state, of the business, making them the natural starting point of corporate finance.

Whereas the profit and loss account shows how well (or not) a company has performed both operationally and financially, the balance sheet displays the company's assets on the left-hand side and how these assets are financed on the right-hand side. Finally, the cash flow statement shows how much cash the business has generated and how much has been used up on operational, investing and financing activities.

. . . TO CORPORATE FINANCE

Accounting is about keeping a record of past performance. By contrast, corporate finance looks into the future. Ultimately, corporate finance provides a set of tools and techniques for deciding how to invest the limited financial resources available today to create value in the future. At the centre of corporate finance is 1) capital budgeting, 2) capital structure and 3) working capital.

1) CAPITAL BUDGETING

Capital budgeting involves the allocation and direction of capital to maximise the return from it. This can be achieved by making sound investments. In its simplest form, an investment is about getting more from a project or an opportunity than what has been put in. Hence, the key is to identify those investments that are beneficial.

Investment criteria

Three popular methods of assessing whether investments can generate gains were introduced in this book: 1) payback, 2) net present value (NPV) and 3) internal rate of return (IRR). The payback approach is simply a matter of deciding whether the period required to recover the initial investment is acceptable. The problem with this method is that it ignores the gains and losses generated after the defined period. It also does not take into account the cost of capital. Ultimately, the other two methods are generally considered to be a more rigorous means of reaching an investment decision.

As an investment criterion, NPV is based on a simple premise: it deducts the initial outlay from all the future gains expressed in today's terms. A positive result (i.e. NPV > 0) means that the future gains outsize the amount put in today, thereby representing the value created by the investment. A negative result (i.e. NPV < 0), by contrast, means that the investment is value-destroying given that the actualised sum of all the gains made in the future does not cover the amount to be invested today.

Compared to NPV, which shows *how much* value is created through an investment decision, IRR – the rate at which the NPV would be 0 – determines whether the return generated can cover the cost of capital (which is also the investors' required return). So, if the IRR of the investment is 30 per cent and the company's cost of capital is 20 per cent, i.e. IRR > weighted average cost of capital (WACC), the investment is deemed to be value-creating.

FCF

To measure real money "value" or "gains", it makes sense to use the free cash flows (FCF) method because this represents the cash that is left after all due charges have been paid or collected. Thus, any leftover money is to be distributed to all the investors (i.e. both the debt providers and the equity shareholders), therefore creating value for them.

FCF are made up of three components: 1) CFO (reflecting the cash flow made from the company's operations; 2) CAPEX (or capital expenditure, representing one-time, unusually large purchases); and 3) change in NWC (or net working capital, the additional money needed to be tied up in order to run day-to-day operations). When calculating FCF, it is of paramount importance to think about whether the cash is coming into (inflow) or out of (outflow) the "briefcase".

M&A and company valuation

Investments commonly come in the form of mergers and acquisitions (M&A). Drivers motivating companies to buy others are 1) operational, 2) industry-specific, 3) strategic, 4) financial or 5) personal.

Similarly to other types of investments, the value of a business or, more precisely, the enterprise value (EV), can be determined by 1) calculating the total discounted FCF that it can generate within the explicit forecast period and 2) estimating the terminal value – the latter being calculated as the sum of all FCF generated forever, beyond the explicit forecast period. This is the basis for the WACC valuation method. Two other common approaches are the industry comparables and M&A comparables methods. Contrary to the WACC method, which looks at how effective a company is at generating money using its assets, these two comparison approaches take an external perspective to assess the value of a business by comparing it to its closest competitors and previous M&A transactions in the industry.

2) CAPITAL STRUCTURE

Companies are financed either by a combination of equity and debt or by equity alone. Since an investment only makes economic sense if it can generate a return that is higher than the cost of the financing going into the investment, businesses need to have a good understanding of how much each type of financing costs. To understand the relationship between the cost of capital and the return required by investors, it is helpful to view them as two sides of the same coin, as shown in Table 9.1.

Debt

Bank loans

There are two main types of debt financing that companies can tap into. First and foremost are bank loans. The interest that the bank

Table 9.1 Two sides of the same coin for different types of financing

Types of financing	From the company's perspective	"The coin"	From the investors' perspective
Bank loans	Cost of using bank loans	Interest rate	Return needed by the bank
Bonds	Cost of using bonds	YTM	Return needed by the bond investors/holders
Equity	Cost of using equity	Dividend growth model or CAPM	Return needed by the shareholders

charges represents the cost that the company has to pay in order to access the loan. From the perspective of the banks, this interest charged represents the return that they are getting from providing the loan. Put differently, the cost of using bank loans is also the return required by the bank to justify the lending.

Bonds

Another option for debt financing, especially for large corporations, is bonds. Every time that a business makes a bond issue or sells bonds, it is effectively borrowing money from the markets. The bondholders − i.e. the investors who buy these bonds − are lending money to the business. They get returns on their investments through: 1) coupons, which can be thought of as the interest paid by the bond, and 2) the difference between the bond price and the face value. The bond price paid by the investors effectively represents the money that they lend to the business (and that the business borrows). The face value − the amount to be returned to the investors when the bond matures − is therefore the amount that the borrowing company pays back to the investors. This is the reason why, even for bonds that pay no coupons (i.e. zero-coupon bonds), investors can make money, as long as they get back more than they lent out in the first place.

One of the biggest difficulties in understanding bonds is the concept of yield to maturity, or YTM. It is important to remember that YTM is *not* the interest rate of the bond. YTM represents the combined return that the investors can get from both the coupons *and* the difference between the bond price and the face value. Flipping to the other side of the coin, the same YTM is what the borrowing company has to pay in order to convince the bond buyers to lend. In other words, for the borrower, YTM is the cost of using the bond.

Equity

Regardless of whether a business takes on debt, it will have to be partially, if not entirely, funded through equity. Determining the cost of using equity often requires estimating the rate of return that shareholders demand.

The dividend growth model

One approach to calculating the cost of equity is the dividend growth model. This method may be simple to use, but its main shortcoming is that it assumes that the company pays dividends and that such dividends will grow forever at a chosen rate. Another issue is that, since it is based on dividends, this model is more relevant to established companies than new ones. This is because new firms that are in their high-growth phase rarely pay dividends, preferring to reinvest the money into the company to fund further growth instead. A more flexible and, seemingly, more rigorous approach that does not rely on these assumptions is the capital asset pricing model, or simply CAPM.

Capital asset pricing model

The underpinning principle of the concept of CAPM lies in the return and risk of a financial asset. Whereas the return refers to how much a person can expect to gain from the investment based on historical performance, risk can be thought of as the chances of *not* being able to obtain this expected gain. Consider a portfolio that contains two companies called Bob and Charlie. The return that the investor could get from holding this portfolio depends on: 1) the return that Bob and Charlie can each provide and 2) the proportion of the investor's capital allocated to Bob and Charlie. Estimating the risk of this portfolio, on the other hand, involves three factors: 1) the risk of investing in Bob and Charlie individually, 2) the proportion of the investor's capital invested in each of them and 3) most importantly, the correlation between Bob and Charlie – that is, the extent to which the returns of Bob and Charlie fluctuate together.

Diversification

According to corporate finance theory, when the two shares are negatively correlated (i.e. when the return on Bob is positive, more frequently than not the return on Charlie is negative), the holder of the portfolio can eliminate a certain amount of risk while still getting a good return – so much so that, if an investor continues to add more assets/investments into their portfolio, even more risk can be eliminated.

Yet, it is impossible to completely be rid of risk through the principle of diversification. Diversification pretty much loses all effect when there are around 25 to 30 assets included in the portfolio. The reason for this is that, while non-systematic risk (risk that is specific to a company) can be eliminated, systematic risk cannot be diversified away by holding a diverse portfolio. This is the case because systematic risk results from the wider business and economic environment, which essentially affects all financial assets. Consequently, regardless of the makeup of a portfolio, it is impossible to eliminate systematic risk.

This observation leads to two important implications. First, financial theorists assume that all investors hold a portfolio to fully diversify all the non-systematic risk away, leaving them exposed to systematic risk only. Second, it is necessary to have a way to measure the systematic risk.

Beta

Beta addresses this second point, as it measures how volatile a company's return is compared to the wider market. In essence, beta shows to what extent a company's share is affected by the general economic and business environment. A beta of 1 means that the company is just as volatile as the wider environment. By the same token, a company with a beta of 1.2 or 0.8 is more or less volatile, respectively, than the market.

The CAPM formula

It is now possible to see what CAPM represents. CAPM is made up of three components: 1) risk-free (r_f) investments that guarantee a small return; 2) beta (β), which measures the systematic risk of a company's return; and 3) market risk premiums ($r_m - r_f$), which represent the additional rewards and return that an investor is getting from taking more risk by putting their money in a share in the market instead of making risk-free investments.

Hence, CAPM portrays the following: when an investor buys a share of, say, Company ABC, she can expect to receive at least the return from her risk-free investments (r_f) and then, on top of this, the rewards from taking the risk of investing in ABC's shares ($r_m - r_f$). Such additional rewards depend on how sensitive the company's return is vis-à-vis the market return (β). The resulting CAPM is therefore the return that the investor needs to obtain in order to justify the extra risk of putting her money into ABC. From ABC's perspective, this same required return represents the company's cost of raising the capital from this shareholder – in short, the cost of equity.

WACC

An investment should only go ahead if the value it can create is higher than the amount of money put in. Put differently, an investment is only attractive when the return that it can provide exceeds the cost of the capital injected. Since a company can source capital from both lenders and shareholders, the cost of capital must reflect the mix of the debt and equity that it has taken on – hence the term WACC. As can be seen in the formula in Figure 9.1, WACC takes into account the respective percentages of debt and equity used by the company, as well as the cost of debt and the cost of equity. Whereas equity does not have tax benefits, a tax shield is applied to the debt portion of capital composition given that the interest is paid before taxes. The resulting WACC can then be used to discount FCF.

3) WORKING CAPITAL

The third concern of corporate finance, in addition to capital budgeting and capital structure, is (net) working capital. This refers to the cash that has to be tied up in order to get the business activities and day-to-day operations going. To run operations, a company often has to pay money "out of its own pocket"; for instance, it may have sold a good but it must wait to be paid (so cash is being tied up). The opposite can also happen: a company may receive its purchases up front but pay for them later. In this case, it holds onto its cash for a bit longer, which means that more cash is available for other business activities.

Since using cash has a cost, managers should actively seek to lower the amount of cash needed for a business operation. They can do so by keeping the amount of money tied up in inventory and accounts receivable to the minimum, while maximising the amount of money in accounts payable.

Last but not least, since NWC is cash that is only tied up in the running of business operations, all the NWC is recovered when an operation comes to an end. In this case, all the NWC outstanding will go back into the "briefcase"!

THE FUTURE OF CORPORATE FINANCE

It is very much hoped that this book has created value for you and that purchasing it has been an NPV-positive investment! The intention of this book was to be a practical resource for newcomers to corporate finance who need to understand its main concepts and the impact it can have on their business and who need to be able to use this understanding in their daily professional activities. This book ends with a quick comment about the future of the field.

Corporate finance is not immune to technological change. Lately, fintech (short for financial technology) has looked increasingly likely to revolutionise the finance industry. Admittedly, in the short term at least, it will not change much of the fundamental principles of corporate finance discussed in this book. Yet, fintech is developing fast, and it is particularly overhauling the back-end operations of financial services companies, as well as the ways in which they engage customers. In the near future, fintech will create greater transparency, more free flow of information and simplified engagement processes in the financial sector and businesses in other industries. All of these developments can help to make us more astute at managing financial affairs.

As an example, more robots/algorithms have recently been developed to automate the management of working capital. These technologies not only calculate how much money is currently being tied up by operations, but they also forecast how much of this capital would be needed in various timeframes in the future. If they anticipated a shortfall, the algorithms would also survey the loans that are available and their conditions in order to identify the ones that would be the most advantageous for the company to take up.

Given these developments, one may question whether there is a need to learn about financial management. Ironically, it is precisely in times of such change that it is ever more important to have a good grasp of the fundamentals of corporate finance. With it, not only are we better equipped to make financial decisions and manage a business, but we are also able to take advantage of the benefits of evolving technologies more quickly. Furthermore, technologies are gradually making corporate financial management – a domain that was once restricted to financial professionals – accessible to a wider number of people. As this field is being democratised, possessing the ability to deal with finance directly without using intermediaries will certainly add value to both our personal and working lives.

INDEX